First World War
and Army of Occupation
War Diary
France, Belgium and Germany

38 DIVISION
Divisional Troops
Royal Army Veterinary Corps
49 Mobile Veterinary Section
4 December 1915 - 31 July 1919

WO95/2550/4

The Naval & Military Press Ltd
www.nmarchive.com
Published in association with The National Archives

Published by

The Naval & Military Press Ltd

Unit 10 Ridgewood Industrial Park,

Uckfield, East Sussex,

TN22 5QE England

Tel: +44 (0) 1825 749494

www.naval-military-press.com

www.nmarchive.com

This diary has been reprinted in facsimile from the original. Any imperfections are inevitably reproduced and the quality may fall short of modern type and cartographic standards.

© Crown Copyright
Images reproduced by permission of The National Archives, London, England, 2015.

Contents

Document type	Place/Title	Date From	Date To
Heading	WO95/2550/4 49 Mobile Veterinary Section		
Heading	38th Division 49th Mobile Vety Secn Dec 1915-Jly 1919		
Heading	38th Div. 49th Mob. Vet. Sec. Vol I Dec 15 Jly 19		
Heading	War Diary Of W Tully Christie Lieut AVC O/C 49th M.V.S. 38th Division From Dec 4th 1915 To Dec 31st 1915 Vol I		
War Diary	Winchester	04/12/1915	04/12/1915
War Diary	Havre	05/12/1915	06/12/1915
War Diary	Rocquetoire	07/12/1915	20/12/1915
War Diary	St Venant	21/12/1915	31/12/1915
Heading	49th Mob. Vet. Sect. Vol. 2 Jan 16		
Heading	War Diary Of W. Tully-Christie Lieut AVC O/C 49th D.V.A. 38th Division From Jan 1 1916 To Jan 31st 1916 Vol II		
War Diary	St. Venant	01/01/1916	28/01/1916
War Diary	Lestrem	29/01/1916	31/01/1916
Heading	49th M.V.S. 38th Div		
War Diary	In The Field N. Lestrem	01/01/1916	29/02/1916
Miscellaneous	D.A.G. G.H.Q. 3rd Echelon	31/03/1916	31/03/1916
Heading	War Diary Of Lieut P. Hussar A.V.C O.C. 49th Mobile Vat Section From March 1st 1916 To March 31st 1916 Volume IV		
War Diary	In The Field Lestrem	01/03/1916	07/03/1916
War Diary	Locon	08/03/1916	31/03/1916
Heading	War Diary of Lieut. P. Howard A.V.C. O.C.49. Mobile Vet. Section From April 1st 1916 To April 30th 1916 Volume V		
War Diary	Locon	01/04/1916	16/04/1916
War Diary	La Gorgue	17/04/1916	29/04/1916
Heading	War Diary of Lieut. P. Howard A.V.C. O.C. 49th Mobile Vet. Section. From May 1st 1916 To May 31st 1916 Volume VI		
War Diary	La Gorgue	01/05/1916	31/05/1916
Heading	War Diary of Lieut P. Howard A.V.C. O.C. 49th Mobile Vet. Section. From June 1st To June 30th 1916 Volume VII		
War Diary	La Gorgue	01/06/1916	12/06/1916
War Diary	Busnes	13/06/1916	14/06/1916
War Diary	Auchel	15/06/1916	15/06/1916
War Diary	St Michel	16/06/1916	26/06/1916
War Diary	Boffles Lanches	27/06/1916	30/06/1916
Heading	War Diary of Lieut P. Howard A.V.C. O.C. 49th Mobile Vet. Section. From July 1st 1916 To July 31st 1916 Volume VIII		
War Diary	Septonville	01/07/1916	02/07/1916
War Diary	Lealvillers	03/07/1916	04/07/1916
War Diary	Treux	05/07/1916	12/07/1916
War Diary	Coisy	13/07/1916	13/07/1916
War Diary	Pont Remy	14/07/1916	15/07/1916

War Diary	Couin	16/07/1916	16/07/1916
War Diary	Famechon	17/07/1916	28/07/1916
War Diary	Sarton	29/07/1916	30/07/1916
War Diary	Esquelbecq	31/07/1916	31/07/1916
Miscellaneous	General Staff, 38th. Division.	01/09/1916	01/09/1916
Heading	War Diary of Capt. P. Howard A.V.C. O.C. 49th Mobile Vet. Section From August 1st 1916 To August 31st 1916 Volume IX		
War Diary	Esquelbecq Station	01/08/1916	10/08/1916
War Diary	Ledringham	11/08/1916	21/08/1916
War Diary	Watou	22/08/1916	30/08/1916
War Diary	War Diary of Capt. P. Howard A.V.C. O.C. 49th Mobile Vet. Section. From Sept 1st 1916 To Sept 30th 1916 Volume X		
War Diary	Watou	01/09/1916	30/09/1916
Heading	War Diary of Capt. P. Howard A.V.C. 49th Mobile Vet Section. From Oct 1st To Oct 31st 1916 Volume XI		
War Diary	Watou	01/10/1916	31/10/1916
Heading	War Diary of Capt. P. Howard A.V.C. 49th Mobile Vet. Section. From Nov. 1st 1916 To Nov 30th 1916 Volume XII		
War Diary	Watou	01/11/1916	30/11/1916
Heading	War Diary of P. Howard Capt. A.V.C. 49th Mobile Veterinary Section. From Dec.1st 1916 To Dec.31st 1916 Volume XIII		
War Diary	Watou	01/12/1916	15/12/1916
War Diary	Ledringhem	16/12/1916	31/12/1916
Heading	War Diary of P. Howard Capt. A.V.C. 49th Mobile Vet. Section. From Jan 1st 1917 To Jan 31st 1917 Volume XIV		
War Diary	Ledringhem	01/01/1917	19/01/1917
War Diary	Watou	20/01/1917	31/01/1917
Heading	War Diary of P. Howard Capt. A.V.C. 49th Mobile Vet. Section. From Feb 1st 1917 To Feb 28th 1917 Volume XV		
War Diary	Watou	01/02/1917	28/02/1917
Heading	War Diary of P. Howard Capt. A.V.C. 49th Mobile Vet. Section. From March 1st 1917 To March 31st 1917 Volume XVI		
War Diary	Watou	01/03/1917	31/03/1917
Heading	War Diary of P. Howard Capt. A.V.C. No. 49 Mobile Vet. Section. From April 1st To April 30th 1917 Volume XVII		
War Diary	Watou	01/04/1917	30/04/1917
Heading	War Diary of Captain P. Howard A.V.C. No. 49 Mobile Vet. Section. From May 1st 1917 To May 31st 1917 Volume XVIII		
War Diary	Watou	01/05/1917	31/05/1917
Heading	War Diary of Capt. P. Howard A.V.C. No. 49 Mobile Vet. Section. From 1st June 1917 To June 30th 1917 Volume XIX		
War Diary	Watou	01/06/1917	15/06/1917
War Diary	Voxvrie	16/06/1917	30/06/1917
Heading	War Diary of Capt. P. Howard A.V.C. No. 49 Mobile Veterinary. Section. From 1st July 1917 To July 31st 1917 Volume XX		

War Diary	Fontes	01/07/1917	16/07/1917
War Diary	Tannay	17/07/1917	17/07/1917
War Diary	Caestre	18/07/1917	18/07/1917
War Diary	Eecke	19/07/1917	19/07/1917
War Diary	Proven	20/07/1917	21/07/1917
War Diary	Voxvrie	22/07/1917	31/07/1917
Heading	War Diary of Capt. P. Howard A.V.C. No. 49 Mobile Veterinary Section. From Aug 1st 1917 To Aug 31st 1917 Vol XXI		
War Diary	Voxvrie	01/08/1917	06/08/1917
War Diary	Proven	07/08/1917	19/08/1917
War Diary	Voxvrie	20/08/1917	31/08/1917
Heading	War Diary of Capt. P. Howard A.V.C. No 49 Mobile Veterinary Section. From Sept 1st 1917 To Sept 30th 1917 Vol XXII		
War Diary	Vox Vrie	01/09/1917	11/09/1917
War Diary	Proven	12/09/1917	13/09/1917
War Diary	Eecke	14/09/1917	14/09/1917
War Diary	Steenbeck	15/09/1917	15/09/1917
War Diary	Epinette	16/09/1917	30/09/1917
Heading	War Diary of Capt. P. Howard A.V.C. No. 49 Mobile Veterinary Section. From Oct.1st To Oct 31st Volume XXIII		
War Diary	Sheet 36 G 14 G 2-4	01/10/1917	31/10/1917
Heading	War Diary of Capt. P. Howard A.V.C. No. 49 Mobile Veterinary Section. From Nov 1st To Nov 30th 1917 Vol XXIV		
War Diary	Sheet 36 C 14 C2.4	01/11/1917	30/11/1917
Heading	War Diary of Capt P. Howard A.V.C. No. 49 Mobile Veterinary Section. From Dec 1st To Dec 31st Vol XXV		
War Diary	Sheet 36 C 14 C2-4	01/12/1917	31/12/1917
Heading	War Diary of Captain P. Howard A.V.C. No. 49 Mobile Veterinary Section. From January 1 To January 31st 1918 Vol XXVI		
War Diary	Sheet 36 C 14 C 2-4	01/01/1918	15/01/1918
War Diary	Regnier-Leclercq	16/01/1918	31/01/1918
Heading	War Diary of Capt. P. Howard A.V.C. No. 49 Mobile Veterinary Section. From Feb 1st To Feb 28th 1918 Vol XXVII		
War Diary	Regnier-Leclercq (Nord)	01/02/1918	16/02/1918
War Diary	Steenwerck	18/02/1918	28/02/1918
Heading	War Diary of Captain A. Young A.V.C. No. 49 Mobile Veterinary Section. From March 1st To March 31st Vol XXVIII		
War Diary	Steenwerck	01/03/1918	30/03/1918
War Diary	Merville	31/03/1918	31/03/1918
Heading	War Diary of Captain. A. Young A.V.C. No. 49 Mobile Vety Section. From April 1st 1918 To April 30th 1918 Vol. XXIX		
War Diary	Merville	01/04/1918	01/04/1918
War Diary	Doullens	02/04/1918	30/04/1918
Heading	War Diary of Capt. A. Young. A.V.C. No. 49 Mobile Veterinary Section. From May 1st 1918 To May 31st 1918 Volume XXX		
War Diary	Toutencourt	01/05/1918	31/05/1918

Heading	War Diary of Captain A. Young. A.V.C. No. 49th Mobile Veterinary Section From June 1st 1918 To June 30th 1918 Vol 31		
War Diary	Toutencourt	01/06/1918	30/06/1918
Heading	War Diary of Capt A. Young. A.V.C. No. 49th Mobile Veterinary Section From July 1st 1918 To July 31st 1918 Vol 32		
War Diary	Toutencourt	01/07/1918	31/07/1918
Heading	War Diary of Capt J Macfarlane A.V.C. 49th Mobile Veterinary Section From Aug 1st To Aug 31st Vol XXXIII		
War Diary	Toutencourt (Somme)	01/08/1918	15/08/1918
War Diary	Toutencourt	16/08/1918	25/08/1918
War Diary	Varennes	26/08/1918	26/08/1918
War Diary	Bouzincourt	27/08/1918	27/08/1918
War Diary	Aveluy	28/08/1918	31/08/1918
Heading	War Diary of Capt J. Macfarlane A.V.C. 49th Mobile Veterinary Section From 1st Sept To 30th Sept 1918 Vol XXXIV		
War Diary	Aveluy	01/09/1918	02/09/1918
War Diary	Contalmaison	03/09/1918	04/09/1918
War Diary	Bazentin-Le-Petit	05/09/1918	09/09/1918
War Diary	Le Transloy	10/09/1918	12/09/1918
War Diary	Rocquigny	13/09/1918	13/09/1918
War Diary	Sheet 57.6. VI.A.8.8	14/09/1918	30/09/1918
Heading	War Diary of Capt J. Macfarlane A.V.C. 49th Mobile Veterinary Section From 1st October To 31st October Volume XXXV		
Miscellaneous	Confidential		
War Diary	Sheet 51C VI.A.8.8	01/10/1918	01/10/1918
War Diary	Fins	02/10/1918	07/10/1918
War Diary	Ossus	08/10/1918	09/10/1918
War Diary	Malincourt	10/10/1918	11/10/1918
War Diary	Bertry	12/10/1918	23/10/1918
War Diary	Troisville	24/10/1918	25/10/1918
War Diary	Montay	26/10/1918	31/10/1918
Heading	War Diary of O.C., 49th Mobile Veterinary Section From 1st. November 1918 To 30th November 1918 Volume XXXVI		
War Diary	Montay	01/11/1918	05/11/1918
War Diary	Wagnonville	06/11/1918	07/11/1918
War Diary	Englefontaine	08/11/1918	08/11/1918
War Diary	Locquinol	09/11/1918	10/11/1918
War Diary	Aulnoye	11/11/1918	30/11/1918
Heading	War Diary of Captain J. Macfarlane R A.V.C. 49th Mobile Veterinary Section From Dec 1st 1918 To Dec 31st 1918 Vol XXXVII		
War Diary	Aulnoye	01/12/1918	11/12/1918
War Diary	Berlaimont	12/12/1918	31/12/1918
War Diary	War Diary of Captain J. Macfarlane R.A.V.C. 49th Mobile Veterinary Section From Jan 1st 1919 To January 31st 1919 Vol XXXVII		
War Diary	Neuvilly	01/01/1919	01/01/1919
War Diary	Masnieres	02/01/1919	02/01/1919
War Diary	Manancourt	03/01/1919	03/01/1919
War Diary	Meaulte	04/01/1919	04/01/1919

War Diary	L.A. Houssoye	05/01/1919	23/01/1919
War Diary	Allonville	24/01/1919	31/01/1919
Heading	War Diary of Captain J. Macfarlane R.A.V.C. 49th Mobile Veterinary Section From Feb 1st 1919 To Feby 28th Vol XXXVIII		
War Diary	Allonville	01/02/1919	28/02/1919
War Diary	War Diary of Captain J. Macfarlane R.A.V.C. 49th Mobile Veterinary Section From March 1st 1919 To March 31st Vol XXXIX		
War Diary	Allonville (Somme)	01/03/1919	31/03/1919
War Diary	Montieres	01/05/1919	31/05/1919
Miscellaneous	O.C. 49th M.V.S	07/08/1919	07/08/1919
War Diary	Montieres	01/06/1919	31/07/1919

WO95/2550/4
49 Mobile Veterinary Section

38TH DIVISION

49TH MOBILE VETY SECN

DEC 1915 - JLY 1919

49th Punj: Vet. deed
Vol I

19/7928

38 M/W

Dec. 15
Gy. 101
3/8

Confidential

War Diary
of
W. Lully. Chocolate Lieut APO
¼ 19th R.W.J
35th Divisions

From Dec 4th 1915 to Dec 31st 1915

Vol. I

Army Form C. 2118.

WAR DIARY
or
INTELLIGENCE SUMMARY.   49th V.1

(Erase heading not required.)

Instructions regarding War Diaries and Intelligence Summaries are contained in F. S. Regs., Part II. and the Staff Manual respectively. Title pages will be prepared in manuscript.

Place	Date	Hour	Summary of Events and Information	Remarks and references to Appendices
Winchester	4/12/15	9.15	Left Winchester for Luddington by road	
		3 pm	Arrived Southampton Dock	
		3.45	Embarked however this Col. Fisher A.D.C. of troops	
		5	History of Offs. & troops on board	
		6	Inspected Ship	
Havre	5/12/15	7.30 am	Arrived Havre	
		8	Disembarked	
		4.45	Marched to No. 5 Rest rest camp	
		2 pm	Ludenforto refreshed	
	6/12/15	3.30 pm	Horse motor lorry off with A.D.C. party	
		4	Left camp from station pl. 3	
		5	Started entraining	
		6.30	Finished entraining	
		8.10	Started from station	
Augustines	7/12/15	3.40 am	Arrived Aire	
		6.15	Detrained	
		7	Arrived at billets, got 4 for horses all good	
	8/12/15	9.30 am	Late C.O. starts	
		11	Inspected Rifles Pkt Wants from below pickets for turning her lorry.	
		3 pm	Inspected Horse RE Lorries & trsp. 105.7°	
		5	Got Start for surveying horses	
	9/12/15	12 md	Sent AF. B103 Army	
		2.30	Letter to Lieut Wards and Daughes pl. them 3955.7 days for knackerhousers	

Army Form C. 2118

WAR DIARY
or
INTELLIGENCE SUMMARY.
(Erase heading not required.)

Instructions regarding War Diaries and Intelligence Summaries are contained in F. S. Regs., Part II. and the Staff Manual respectively. Title pages will be prepared in manuscript.

Place	Date	Hour	Summary of Events and Information	Remarks and references to Appendices
	10/12/15	11 a.m.	Drew Pay 5/10.6.0	
		2.30 pm	Found Mess	
		3	A.D.S offices with release for sick	
	11/12/15	10 a.m.	Got billet papers punched	
		11	Inspected stable with A.D.S	
		3 p.m.	Received 3 horses from Lieut. Townsend A.V.C	
	12/12/15	10 a.m.	A.D.S personnel left arrived in M.T.	
		11	8 horses from Lieut Townsend A.V.C	
		2.30 pm	A.D.S Arrived. Informed his that horses of Lahore Division will come to Sec	
		3	Lieut wen R.T.O Wilson	
		4	Sent down to Aire to pick up R.F.A horse transport	
		6	Inspected 8 horses to send off tomorrow	
	13/12/15	6 a.m.	Sent 8 horses to Sup Chole	
		10	10 horses and mules from Lahore Division	
		12	All in yard and being brought and fed	
		3 pm	Gave transport over to Major Hepburn Army Vet.	
		4	2 more Horses in from Lieut Townsend	
		6.30	Shut roll and reported to A.D.S	
	14/12/15	8.30 am	Received 24 Horses 3 mules to base Hospital	
		9	Inspected billets	
		11	Inspected all sick horse	
		2 pm	A.D.S. Office	
		4	Office Sut reports Farcothril	

Army Form C. 2118

WAR DIARY
or
INTELLIGENCE SUMMARY.
(Erase heading not required.)

Instructions regarding War Diaries and Intelligence Summaries are contained in F. S. Regs., Part II. and the Staff Manual respectively. Title pages will be prepared in manuscript.

Place	Date	Hour	Summary of Events and Information	Remarks and references to Appendices
	15/12/15	a.m. 9.30	Lieut Abbot killed and Lt Ck Harris	
		10.30	A Bns Office.	
		11.10	Sgt Checkland returned after having carried Lieut 6.0m 13.12.15 wounded & finishing	
			return of orders from R.F.A.	
		12.30p	3 horses in from 2nd Lowland Bgd R.F.A. one down, 2 superficial harness.	
		2	At orders received office	
		4	Moved to Lyt.	
	16/12/15	8am	Lieut Sgt S Thomas with Sgt Checkland	
		9	Received 5 am with 5 for the Iron Field 19 Rmt	
		10.30	Pt Powell 73. and W Kelly 1203 Lot. moved refract A.D.V.S	
		11	purposes and killed and sick Horses	
		12	At A.D.M.S. Kelly and horses from Hospital	
		2pm	2 horses in 1 from L.R.H. L.R.H.4	
		3.15	at A Bns Office	
		4.45	2 horses Lame 16 W.R.W.7. 42 Lieut Stewart	
	17/12/15	9.0 am	Asing farrier dane castiating B.2000. B 231	
		10	Powell and Kelly off to Hospital	
		10.30	Lieutenant killed Lieut Stewart	
		11	A Bns Office.	
		12	Any Hrse, one Mare J.2.30.00	
		12.45p	Officer got all reports done	
		3	Lieut kill the Mare	
			at A.O.D.s Office for conference with V.O. Howard & Lieut Busey R.7A	
		3.30	received Lithographs in Glanders	
		4	At transport lines, from H.Q.C	
		4.30	Sent A.F.B.213 off	
		11.30	Received some H.Q. re refacting at C.Bn Transport	

2353 Wt. W3544/1454 700,000 5/15 D. D. & L. A.D.S.S./Forms/C. 2118.

WAR DIARY or INTELLIGENCE SUMMARY

Army Form C. 2118

Instructions regarding War Diaries and Intelligence Summaries are contained in F.S. Regs., Part II. and the Staff Manual respectively. Title pages will be prepared in manuscript.

(Erase heading not required.)

Summary of Events and Information

Place	Date	Hour	Summary of Events and Information	Remarks and references to Appendices
	19/7/15	9 am	Reported at A.A. Offices H.Q. 10 minutes carrying on. Lieut Owens and Lieuman A.S.C. with 6 ORs there to orders given	
		10.45	and went to draw ten lewis Horses and one Hackney R.F.A. Lame c.26	
		11.30	18 horses on train went horses R.F.A. and 38th Division	
		12	In from Lt. Owen 0.C. 1005 Lieut 18 H.Q. m. it unloading horses at B.Ryan	
		12.30	Lieut Owen A.S.C. 1005 Lieut 18 H.Q. to R.T.O.	
		3	Down to S.R.A.O.S. Revived back u. 4 yellow cases and tramway lane	
		6.15	Told S.R.A.O.S. Revived back on duty low lives over till the start	
		6.30	Intelligence returned of the King over lives over till the start 1st four gall. afternoon	
		7.30	Lieut Owen Reported to unit. Train in two pieces R.F.A. from 38th Division	
		11	Lent for London R.F.A. horses from 38th Division	
			arrive 65 Lift Brook	
			went in sick horses from ran and	
20/7/15	8.30	days wished to 5ft Brooks	
		12	Lieut 32 Horses to King Edward	
		1	Ol. AOUS	
		3	Interpreters returned A.O.vs to It. Humbert Billets	
		8	Interpreter returned halling done	
23/7/15	9 am	went off from 26th Warrant All the billets taken by other unit. We had to try where	
	12.15	Arrived 26 Warrant All the billets taken by other unit. We had to try where w/off. They all very from two properly sick. The list write left them very	
			dirty. Also two got all they have had lever found till 4.30 we got	
			their all wreck. Owen	
	6 pm	At MOUs offices find that a large number of horses have been left where	
			by out of them down to I should have to go and get them all in	
24/7/15	10 am	At AOUs office till 12.30 getting out about horses left behind	
	5.30	At AOUs offices till 6/m	
26/7/15	10 —	At AOUs office two new orders in	
	11.30	At Hqtrs. C.Q.M.G. to report not off on the horse have to meet Lt Wooley before	
			getting orders At two all they there Wooley. Taking all wounded to Lane Rept London	
			time on change of Billets	

Army Form C. 2118

WAR DIARY
or
INTELLIGENCE SUMMARY.
(Erase heading not required.)

Instructions regarding War Diaries and Intelligence Summaries are contained in F.S. Regs., Part II. and the Staff Manual respectively. Title pages will be prepared in manuscript.

Place	Date	Hour	Summary of Events and Information	Remarks and references to Appendices
	24/1/15	4.30	A.D.O.W.S office	
		5—	At HQ received orders re picking up Heavy horses	
	23/1/15	9am	Ticketed all day bad Chill	
		11.30	M.O. in with med.	
		3pm	M.O. in with med.	
	24/2/15 10am		Got all kinds of free work done	
		11.20	Sent Scouts with riders	
		3pm	Sent to see about Charring Horses crew Flour	
	25/2/15 10am		went to see Charring Horse & will turn about Horses for the Floor; Interpreter and 250 Francs to the Charring Station	
		12	A.D.W.S went met with Interprete Forage. Est. F1.00 with act. Cont.	
		2	Interpreter off to the about Forage.	
		3	Interpreter found Forage.	
		4.30	to A.D.W.S till 6 pm	
	26/2/15 10am		got all office Billets done	
		11.30	to A.D.W.S.	
		2	Saw (Sick) Mule on road to station sent 6 horses to have	
		3	A.D.W.S got Float from F3.00 sent Jack to Poincy in train & unload	
		4.5	Train took came at 6.30	
	25/2/15 9am		At A.D.W.S office till 6.30	
			went Talington and Left Break with 8 men to collect the Horses & Eff. gave runner	
			from 1st	
		10.30	Train Load Leaving 19th F.5A	
		6.15	Plenty trouble from Eddleberry Stray horses	
	29/2/15.10.		A.D.W.S Here	
		11	Drew Pay for the Mens F295.00	
		12	Got lighter furnished.	
		2.30	Finished all of mens.	
			Paid over N/R 461.462.	
		3.30	Got attacks furnished	

Army Form C. 2118

WAR DIARY
or
INTELLIGENCE SUMMARY
(Erase heading not required.)

Instructions regarding War Diaries and Intelligence Summaries are contained in F. S. Regs., Part II. and the Staff Manual respectively. Title Pages will be prepared in manuscript.

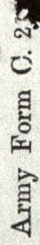

Place	Date	Hour	Summary of Events and Information	Remarks and references to Appendices
	28/11/15	5	At Adv. S. Office	
	29/11/15	10	A day in	
		10.30	Sent party to bury troops.	
		12	Heard from Z.A.D.	
		4	Got back from burying troops	
		10	Regiment ordered off, sent by bus out of billeting area, ducks had think there	
			to any change in Battn: reported to 42pm.	
			At Adv S/Office	
	30.11.15	P.	At Adv. Office	
	31.12	10	Return in town.	
	15	12	Got Street for true Horse Fr.	
		1.30	Sent to Adv. Office	
		3	At Adv. Office	

Willoughby-Christie
Lieut Col
C.O. 57 D.D.

1875 Wt. W593/826 1,000,000 4/15 J.B.C. & A. A.D.S.S./Forms/C.2118.

49th Indl: Ves. Sect.
Vol: 2
Pan 16.

38

Confidential

War Diary

J. A. Scully-Clerke Lieut Col
O.C. 1st Bn. H.L.I.
38th Division

From June 1. 1916
To June 31st Oct 1916

Vol II

Army Form C. 2118

WAR DIARY
or
INTELLIGENCE SUMMARY

49th F.A. / 37th Division

(Erase heading not required.)

Instructions regarding War Diaries and Intelligence Summaries are contained in F. S. Regs., Part II. and the Staff Manual respectively. Title Pages will be prepared in manuscript.

Place	Date	Hour	Summary of Events and Information	Remarks and references to Appendices
ST VENANT	1.1.16	9 a.m.	Wet cold windy.	
		10	Gen. All officer turn out church.	
		12	Hand in form 122 RFA	
		3	Lieut Armstrong RAMC on a sick horse	
		4.30	At O.D.V.S. No smoker. Hope we are in time to float. Attached to us.	
	2.1.16	9 am	We came to col will West	
		10	Enrolment Sgt Brooks ext. Rgy hors. M.H.	
		12	Reformed that but of hay was built. Three another horse knits even the place out	
		4	Wish it was the good sin the C.O.B. tell forward out.	
			detro affected his orderly	
		8	Searched dogs returned	
	3.1.16	9 am	Sent report CRO/52 13.12.15	
		10	By far too wind and chill. Warm	
		11	as Evans clearing stables trust.	
		2	Sent off two horses if Rent B	
		5	At O Div office	
	4.1.16	10.30	Given Rgy from the Base	
		12.30	Sgt Elder preserved	
		1	I know no dirty time day hot especially	
			Kept there 2/180.00"	
		3.30	Came on Dry wet	
	5.1.16	4.45	A.C. MOVE effect	
		9	New auction	
		9.30	Wind. the N.E. on Roll with horses. Moved for stable on one time head.	
		10	Empared C we Some form DADVS	
		12	Letter furnished.	
		1.30	Lieut 19Hammer 3 weeks Gimmel	
		2	Horse at 115 Pugd through of place.	
		2.30	Sgt Brock demand retired.	
		4	At ADVS office	
	6.1.16		Lieut Littlefield to LESTREM	
		11	Arrive there horse and mule	
		12	furnished letters	

Army Form C. 2118.

WAR DIARY
or
INTELLIGENCE SUMMARY.
(Erase heading not required.)

Instructions regarding War Diaries and Intelligence Summaries are contained in F. S. Regs., Part II. and the Staff Manual respectively. Title pages will be prepared in manuscript.

Place	Date	Hour	Summary of Events and Information	Remarks and references to Appendices
ST. VENANT.	6..1.16	3	Left advance report guard guard	
		5	ADMS office	
	7.1.16	9	Pay parade	
		10	Report from Lt. Shackland on last visit	
		17	N.C. 13260. 13213 Dent	
		3	Lt. ADMS office. Resumed on all papers re Capt Shackland	
		5	Wire from 22 NH Rose Pavement	
		9	Letter from DDMS	
	8..1.16	9	Pay from Quart Master	
		10	Arranged typed papers ADMS	
		11	At ADMS office re Weekly returns	
		3	Own in office afternoon	
		3.30	Warned to march. Issued orders effect by Force	
		4	Close down for Lille	
	9.1.16	9	Pay from Lille Col.	
		10	Lille Received to P.M. re ambulance roll	
		12	Lunched officers mess	
		3	At ADMS office. See. Enquired re Capt Shackland. Was told L.28 Convinced fit duty	
			New Sir Same class Lt. Shackland. Did work few more weeks and usual	
			Then Sucrist—	
	10.1.16	5	In my office	
			Saw Lieut Col.	
		9	9 worked in ?	
			Got Letter from Shackland	
		11	Pair from R.T.O.Lt. Shackland	
		2	At ADMS office	
	11.1.16	9	" " " " "	
		10.30	All NCO sent to try the new method of hallow letters	
		11	Col. Finnlow ADMS like week All Day work.	
		12	All leaves from list	
		1	Office closed 4 ?	
		1.30	Self went to Col.	

Army Form C. 2118.

WAR DIARY
or
INTELLIGENCE SUMMARY.
(Erase heading not required.)

Instructions regarding War Diaries and Intelligence Summaries are contained in F. S. Regs., Part II. and the Staff Manual respectively. Title pages will be prepared in manuscript.

Place	Date	Hour	Summary of Events and Information	Remarks and references to Appendices
St Venant				

Army Form C. 2118

WAR DIARY
or
INTELLIGENCE SUMMARY
(Erase heading not required.)

Instructions regarding War Diaries and Intelligence Summaries are contained in F. S. Regs., Part II. and the Staff Manual respectively. Title Pages will be prepared in manuscript.

IV

Place	Date	Hour	Summary of Events and Information	Remarks and references to Appendices
St Venant	17.1.16	1.30	Sent Orderly over 9.194.10.1.16	
		3	Lt ABond reported to Hqrs. Unable—applied to return to Engrs.	
		5.30	Lt offset from ambience	
	18.1.16	9	W.D. and total	
		10	Pte Buckley to Hospital. Reported to ADSV. Brot amb home A.F. B/22	
		11	Lardner gone away	
		12	Townshend office at work	
		2	Enotts shot Rifles rept. Gas helmets	
		3.30	A Division 12.1 RFA	
		4	ADMS 38th AD 2nd 1/94th Amb	
	19.1.16	5	in office	
		1.30	Pair reviews — don't hurry out after horses	
		10	Leave to Chasseurs by Leftt Wright	
		10.30	M.O. Lunch in car Bullock horses all well	
		11	Attempted about horses for floor pour brancardien	
		12	Pulling dang oxen in jaws	
		1	Forming QS Division CO	
		3	Wire to Dunlop for horses	
	20.1.16	4.30	Country look	
		5	At Crows	
		9	Snow news	
		10	Letts from Floor but it was out	
		11	Lord to Bethune	
		11.30	Read Reut x, 6 orders to march	
		1	Sent suit from D.RO15.St	
		1.30	Away Bonne plain	
		4.30	Lt A/Borg offrs	
	21.1.16		all well	
		10.30	View Bay for men	
		1	Bound floor	
		3	A. offrs.	
			total time	
	22.1.16	9	office	
		10		
		3	Lt A/Brs Asst. Adj Inspector	

Army Form C. 2118

WAR DIARY
or
INTELLIGENCE SUMMARY

(Erase heading not required.)

Instructions regarding War Diaries and Intelligence Summaries are contained in F. S. Regs., Part II. and the Staff Manual respectively. Title Pages will be prepared in manuscript.

Place	Date	Hour	Summary of Events and Information	Remarks and references to Appendices
ST VENANT	22.1.16	5	Lunch prepared for have gone front	
			office	
	23.1.16	9	Gen. Hunt gave way plans	
		10	Capt. Hewitt	
		12	Officers Work done	
		1	Officers lectures in	
		5	at GOC's and Behoched a horses 1.5.12.1E	
	24.1.16	5	at P.T.O. w R.E. Heave	
		9	Call G. col. H.Q. Heave	
		10	(Horses in	
		12	Lunch 22 horses off	
		1	Officers weight peut	
		3	Col. Edler Lunch	
	25.1.16	9	Gent Col. at pourent	
		10	Inspected Billets	
		12	A.D.M.S. in Court at 11:45 am the A.S.M.	
		3	Col. Bone Army O.C. 3? at the 2nd ev.	
	26.1.16	9	Lunt Buriat	
		11	Horses & Hernaas in	
		1	Officer's mount	
	27.1.16		Well over to LESTREM	
		11.30	Lunate off here Hillets & very formal	
		1.30	Arrived Get here Billets & very formal	
		4.30	Her offer is getting return Heave	
		6	Sgt Park arrived	
	28.1.16	9	Sent.	
		10	Gave Man twing	
		1.30	Pony reny	
		1.30	Rifle Inspection	
		3	a.D.M.S. office	
		5	Officers mount	

VI Army Form C. 2118

WAR DIARY
or
INTELLIGENCE SUMMARY
(Erase heading not required.)

Instructions regarding War Diaries and Intelligence Summaries are contained in F.S. Regs., Part II. and the Staff Manual respectively. Title Pages will be prepared in manuscript.

Place	Date	Hour	Summary of Events and Information	Remarks and references to Appendices
LESTREM	29.1.16	9	Drill	
		10	Inspection billets	
		10.15	Route march from horses	
		12	Walked to MERVILLE	
		3	Officer's march	
	30.1.16	9	Drill. Very cold.	
		10	Handed command over to Lieut. Howard Q.V.O.	
		12	Trench Work	
	31.1.16	9	Drill Cold	
		1.10	Transfer NEUF CHATELLE	

Confidential

49th M.V.S.
38th Div

War Diary of Capt. Aban. 1. F. Ave. Vol. 3.
6.49th M.V.S.

From Jan 31st 1916. To Feb 29th 1916.

Vol III

WAR DIARY or INTELLIGENCE SUMMARY

Army Form C. 2118

(Erase heading not required.)

Place	Date	Hour	Summary of Events and Information	Remarks and references to Appendices
In the Field N. Lahem	Jan. 31st '16	10 A.M.	I took over command of this 49th M.U.S. from Lieut. Colonel Chisholm A.V.C.	
		5 p.m.	Inspecting the White Stretcher funeral train.	
	Feb. 1st	9 A.M.	Arrange to hire float from MERVILLE. Also Mineurs & H.Q. Have to draw same from Div. Train	
			ye Berlin toddy huts & float of its own.	
		5 p.m.	Advice A.D.V.S. of the hire of a Float. also a microscope.	
	Feb. 2nd	5 p.m.	Have been during Office work most of the day.	
	Feb. 3rd	5 p.m.	Have just Inspects 19. Sick horse at MERVILLE fr No.13. Vet Hospital 3 wires have to be Red-	
			-ins. R.T.O. no V.C. Hospital & no D.D.V.S.	
	Feb. 4th	5 p.m.	Indents for materials for indiv. horse standing Recd R.O.271 to the hon Athurs Conference of	
			V.O.'s at A.D.V.S. Office	
	Feb. 5th	10 A.M.	Inspects by Two outposts at LOEON & LA. Foux. This latter is very poor.	
		2 p.m.	Inspects the Divisional Laundry	
	Feb. 6th	10 A.M.	Inspects No.3 Section Rescue Park. Three horses are looking better	
	Feb. 7th	5 p.m.	Unceds 16. Horses at MERVILLE	
	Feb. 8th	12 p.m.	Inspects yeomanry Outposts	
		5 p.m.	Routine Office work.	
	Feb. 9th	9 A.M.	Driver Fowler. A.S.C. has been sent to Hospital Sick. Inspects Outposts	
	Feb. 10th	5 p.m.	Unceds 19. Sick horses fr MERVILLE	
	Feb. 11th	5 p.m.	Office work & in afternoon attended Conference at A.D.V.S. Office	
	Feb. 12th	5 p.m.	Sent a horse (indendable) fr 13th France to Mr. MACRON. BETHUNE. (as D.D.V.S. Order)	

WAR DIARY
or
INTELLIGENCE SUMMARY
(Erase heading not required.)

Army Form C. 2118

Place	Date	Hour	Summary of Events and Information	Remarks and references to Appendices
In the Field N: Eschun	Feb 13	5 p.m.	Rifle inspection of men. Capt. Bmos A.V.C. B, 1st M.U.S. visits me. Explains new things to be attended to.	
	Feb 14	9 A.M.	Just received notification that by default is to be removed. Wrote strong protest through A.D.V.S.	
		5 p.m.	Capt. Stiddles above W/c to ABBEVILLE to have float in exchange for one of my S.S. tanks draflone. I have him written orders & 8 day rations. Inspected outpost.	
	Feb 15	5 p.m.	Evacuate 16 sick horses from MERVILLE. Return horses about Aquitaine R.M. to New Plac. 1915.	
	Feb 16	5 p.m.	Received Microscope from A.O.V.S.	
	Feb 17	5 p.m.	Inspects 4 squads & Reserve Park. Also outpost hrs off legs.	
	Feb 18	5 p.m.	Presiding veterinary & surgeon of V. O. at A.D.V.S. office. Pte Shadwich has hurt left leg has charge of men & horses & 8 dep. A.P.C. Pte himself in the same charge. S. dep.	
			with light duty. I find him 9 days pay & 9 dep. e.e.	
			for 17 days e.e.	
	Feb 19	5 p.m.	Routine office work in morning. Visits Veterinary officer. See Gives up outpost at FOSSE.	
	Feb 20	5 p.m.	Returns by Squ R.F.A. Below to their Hut. 1. 20 R.F.A. under for A.D.V.S.	
	Feb 21	11 A.M.	Pte Shadwich to harness today in order to shoe. I tell him that under aint.	
	Feb 22	5 p.m.	Evacuates 16. horses thy allione to ABBEVILLE. Float arrived today very first one also a H.D horse.	
	Feb 23	5 p.m.	A.D.V.S. Cause my to try Pt Shadwich. The latter takes to a e.M.	
	Feb 24	12.N.	Inspects him Office tails in after. Inspects Reserve Park. Outpost.	
	Feb 25	5 p.m.	My New Float H.D. horse not filled by heavy accident for M/c Car. No or seems to become during first by e.M. on Pt Shadwich. Inference V.O. at A.O.V.S. office. Feeling vy tired Mrs has littell to day.	
	Feb 26		At MERVILLE also Chang & indentifying which they know.	
	Feb 27		Evacuates 11 horses to NEUF CHATEL. Inspects the Men.	

WAR DIARY
or
INTELLIGENCE SUMMARY
(Erase heading not required.)

Army Form C. 2118

Place	Date	Hour	Summary of Events and Information	Remarks and references to Appendices
In the Field No. Belgium	Feb 27th	12 A.M.	Imperial takes the A.P.M. proceeding in Mr. Shadwicks van to Guilty. Stations 2 months imprisonment without labour less 1 calum Comments by Confirming Officer to 56 Div. F.P. No 1.	
	Feb 28th	5 p.m.	Rifle inspection of men. In afternoon visits A.D.v.S Office & Outpost saw A.P.M. about the carrying out of Shadwicks Sentence.	
	Feb 29th	3 p.m.	Shadwick Sent in to front Command 88th Division. German Aeroplane was brought down just opposite my billet & crashed 12 houses of NEUF CHATEL.	

Jew Morison Lt Col
49th D.V.S.
B.E.F.

D.A.G.
G.H.Q.,
3rd. Echelon.

> A.D.V.S.,
> 38th (WELSH)
> DIVISION.
> No. 1931/16
> Date. 31-3-16

Attached please find Original War Diary of O.C. 49th. Mobile Veterinary Section, for period March 1916, Volume 4.

Frederick Gavin
Major. A.V.C.

31/3/1916.   A.D.V.S. 38th. (Welsh) Division.

49 M Vet
See
Vol. 4

CONFIDENTIAL

WAR DIARY.

of

Lieut. P. Hansens A.V.C.
O.C. 49th Mobile Vet Sect.

From March 1st 1916
To March 31st 1916

(Volume 10)

WAR DIARY
or
INTELLIGENCE SUMMARY

(Erase heading not required.)

Army Form C. 2118

Instructions regarding War Diaries and Intelligence Summaries are contained in F. S. Regs., Part II. and the Staff Manual respectively. Title Pages will be prepared in manuscript.

Place	Date	Hour	Summary of Events and Information	Remarks and references to Appendices
In the Field Lahure	1915 March 1st	5 p.m	Officer took up duty of day. S.S. Hughes arrived for duty	
	2nd	5 p.m	Inspects the Yeomanry & 19 Rear's Park. Preparing return for A.D.V.S.	
	3rd	6 p.m	Attends Conference	
	4th	1 p.m	Officer took. Inspects Yeomany, etc. Visited 460 at A.D.V.S. Office	
	5th	5 p.m	Horse of 157 R.F.A. dies in front. Will bring horse up to Sedin. Evacuate 20 horses at MERVILLE to-day	
	6th	5 p.m	Had rifle inspection to-day. Also horses to by transport begins clearing up	
	7th	8 p.m	Sedin moved preparing to move	
	8th	9 p.m	Very busy to-day, firing the section up. Also evacuate 10 horse at BETHUNE. from LESTREM to LOEON.	
LOE ON	9th	5 p.m	Officer took. Preparing return to-day.	
	10th	5 p.m	Lieut CHAPMAN has give 7 days e.e. home. Issue to a N.E.6	
	11th	5 p.m	Inspects Yeomany. Thinks by its billet at LESTREM.	
	12th	5 p.m	Evacuate 19 horse to-day at BETHUNE. 9 horse When we	

Army Form C. 2118

WAR DIARY
or
INTELLIGENCE SUMMARY
(Erase heading not required.)

Instructions regarding War Diaries and Intelligence Summaries are contained in F. S. Regs., Part II. and the Staff Manual respectively. Title Pages will be prepared in manuscript.

Place	Date	Hour	Summary of Events and Information	Remarks and references to Appendices
LOOON	March 12th	5pm	Veterinary Care of the Gr XI Corps + Officer XI Corps.	
	13th	5pm	Visits BETHUNE. Hospital. Sure Path to Franklin. visits XI Corps + 1st Range Path.	
	14th	5pm	Proceeds 15 Sick Horses at BETHUNE. Arranges to have another Path to get Sure & three sick horses to the station.	
	15th	5pm	D.D.V.S. visits Sadin	
	16th	5pm	D.D.V.S. A.M.S. Army + A.D.V.S. inspects the Sadin	
	16th	11am	16 Horses evacuated today at BETHUNE. Dr HORNE. PE HORNE. awards 2 dogs C.C.	
	17th	5pm	Observed Day. Inspection at A.D.V.S. Office.	
	18th	6pm	Inspects Mule Unit. Rifle Inspection	
	19th	6pm	14 Horses evacuated at BETHUNE.	
	20th	5pm	Inspects the Unit	
	21st	5pm	Saddle Inspection	
	22nd	5pm	Horse Inspection for Brigade for making & Standards	
	23rd	—	Evacuates 16 Horses at BETHUNE.	
	24th	5pm	Q'rs hear M.V.S. visits Dental Hospital LESTREM	
	25th	5pm	Rifle Inspection	

WAR DIARY
or
INTELLIGENCE SUMMARY

Army Form C. 2118

Place	Date	Hour	Summary of Events and Information	Remarks and references to Appendices
LILLON	March 26th	9 p	Received an Infant Mascote to send Plezat to have little Intube £ at 7 pm. Had to cholorform in arrival.	
	27th	9 p	Visits 19 k R.P. Awards Pte PEARCE Aue Ndup £ f Sidens	
	28th	5 p	Returns 8 9.S to a/tens for A.S.C +Fields from Bickent MERVILLE	
	29th	6 p	Fields Amther Gun bullets from MERVILLE have gleared Suspects Visit Yaunny with A.D.v.S.	
	30th	5 p	Quesends 80 Sick have at BETHUNE Apm inspects With Yaunny with A.D.v.S. + Sent in 92 hours to the Section	
	31st	5 p	Conference of V.O.o at A.D.v.S office	

XXXVIII
49 MVS 38 Div
Vol 5

CONFIDENTIAL

WAR DIARY.
of.
Lieut. P. Howard. A.V.C.
o.c. 4.9. Mobile Vet. Section.

From April 1st 1916.
To April 30th 1916.

(Volume V.)

WAR DIARY
or
INTELLIGENCE SUMMARY

(Erase heading not required.)

Army Form C. 2118

Instructions regarding War Diaries and Intelligence Summaries are contained in F.S. Regs., Part II. and the Staff Manual respectively. Title Pages will be prepared in manuscript.

Place	Date	Hour	Summary of Events and Information	Remarks and references to Appendices
L. of C.	April 1st	5 p	Evacuate 24 horses at BETHUNE. The first were winter lame. Inspects Units L. pups. Gave the men a rest in the afternoon.	
	2nd		Visits Sick lines at Stables at 4 p.m.	
	3rd		Lecture in the evening. Equipment inspection at 2 p.m.	
	4th		Evacuate 13 sick horses at BETHUNE.	
	5th		Inspect of Sick lines & Saddlery	
	6th	8 p	Inspection by D.D.V.S. of No. 3. Sat in Remount Park. The horses did not look half the class horses with them.	
	7th		Wind very bad - places with them.	
	8th	6 p	Inspection of 49th Middx by D.D.V.S. & D.D.R. anything seems satisfactory. the D.D.V.S. which is due to be Ratified the Lives in the accident appearance of anything.	
	9th	5 p	Evacuate 20 horses & 8 mules. A.D.V.S. up to day for leave.	
	10th		Bath for Men. Visits 17th Remount Park. & picks out 19 horses (from) for men it is very hot.	
	11th		to drive into the S.E. there my views in treacherousship.	
			Inoculate (Para Typhoid) of A.I.N.C.S. 14 men of Section	
	12th		Inspects 17th Remount Park	
	13th		Evacuate 24 Sick horses. Inspects L, Pups Units	
	14th		Conference at A.D.V.S. (Capt Budge).	

WAR DIARY or INTELLIGENCE SUMMARY

Army Form C. 2118

Place	Date	Hour	Summary of Events and Information	Remarks and references to Appendices
Estaires	April 15th	9 p.m	Visits LA GORGUE. Met O.C. 3rd M.v.S. Re taking over from him the Mens' billets seen little than here. News At 5 p.m. have received an infant wants to bus my float fr a sick man (lame) I took when at 9-45 p.m. with him, bottle out & by the light of my electric torch was unable to diagnose when he been lame	
	April 16th	5 p	Quards 19 sick huses	
	17th	5 p	Billets taken over from 3rd M.v.S. gave this letter a certificate that I told them billets were in a clean sanitary condition. Mrs Seeing's Servis from O.E. so is Mrs.	
La Gorgue	18th	5p	Rifle Inspection of Men A.D.v.S return from leave	
	19th	5p	Inspects Amm. train transport A.S.C. horses look fairly well	
	20th	5p	1st Inspection of Return also horses of Yeomanry. horses look very poor. A/L/CPl.	
			Panter permits to fall sick from 21/3/16. A.D.v.S. inspects this horse billets with apparent satisfaction	
	21st	5p	Man pores. Pte STROWICK Whears from Debility	
	22nd	5p	The I.M.E.D. & 4 been received this is dues of reserve	
	24th		Received 19 sick horses. Inspected by A.D.v.S. & will Yaman & Ant horse transport	

Army Form C. 2118

WAR DIARY
or
INTELLIGENCE SUMMARY
(Erase heading not required.)

Instructions regarding War Diaries and Intelligence Summaries are contained in F. S. Regs., Part II. and the Staff Manual respectively. Title Pages will be prepared in manuscript.

Place	Date	Hour	Summary of Events and Information	Remarks and references to Appendices
La Gorgue April	25th	6pm	Remittance Form. b.1727. forwards to Base in respect of remittance of £40 to Pr [illegible]	
	26th	8pm	Inspected the R.C.s granary. MRIGHT	
	28th	5pm	Conference of V.O.s at A.D.V.S. calls to base camp of Div at Vanney [illegible] Review Front line at 5-30 p.m. my bus has	
	29th	5pm	R. arrived at LA GORGUE 13 hours late. [illegible]	

Pen/Amer: Vc. Av.e.
b.e. 49 to Mob. Vet. Section

1875 Wt. W593/826 1,000,000 4/15 J.B.C. & A. A.D.S.S./Forms/C. 2118.

SECRET.

49 MVS
vol 6
XXXVIII

ORIGINAL CONFIDENTIAL WAR DIARY.
of
Lieut. P. Howard. A.V.C.
O.C.
49th MOBILE VET. SECTION.

(Volume VI)

From May 1st 1916. To May 31st 1916.

Army Form C. 2118

WAR DIARY
or
INTELLIGENCE SUMMARY
(Erase heading not required.)

Instructions regarding War Diaries and Intelligence Summaries are contained in F. S. Regs., Part II. and the Staff Manual respectively. Title Pages will be prepared in manuscript.

Place	Date	Hour	Summary of Events and Information	Remarks and references to Appendices
LA GORGUE	May 1st	6 p	From Mar. of the Relief here unintimates to day	
	2nd		Oxford Public life here Le Boulogne & filed a line Inspects Rnd Will Yeomanry	
	3rd	4:45	Recruits 15 Horses & 1 Mule at LA GORGUE.	
	4th		Purchase of V.O's at A.O.V.S. Office Range Men & Relin	
	5th	6:30	Mule 2 OWARDS A.S.C. Rehits to A.D.g.D: CHAPMAN returns to 33rd & A.S.C.	
	6th	7:50	Ripnd PANTER returns from BOULOGNE into two horses	
	7th		Inspects R. L. Yeomanry Drills - men & Relin at 2 p.m.	
	8th	8:12	Recruits & 13 Horses & Mules at LA GORGUE.	
	9th		Had the Yeomans little white animals.	
	10th			
	11th		Brig Gen Ki(?) & myself for Recruits. Me drills at 2 p.m. Returns him at 4-30 p.m.	
	12th		Purchase at V.O's at A.D.V.S. Office. Inspects Ant. three thought. Co	
	13th		Inwards A.F.O.1727 Returns at 2 p.m. & hurts in 9 horses.	
	14th		Church Parade 9—3. A.M.	
	15th		Returns here at 4-30 p.m.	
	16th		Horse sick here. Also a foal. Mar has foot drill at 2 p.m.	
	17th		Horses & Saddle inspection. Purchases 13 horses & 9 mules.	
	18th		Grant's Drill at 6 A.M. Foot Drill at 2 p.m.	
	19th		Conference A.O.V.S. & pais the Man.	

WAR DIARY
or
INTELLIGENCE SUMMARY
(Erase heading not required.)

Army Form C. 2118

Place	Date	Hour	Summary of Events and Information	Remarks and references to Appendices
LA GORGUE	May 20	5 p.m.	Relieve the Section at 2 p.m.	
	21st		Church Parade at 9.15 A.M.	
	22nd		Medical Inspection at 9 A.M. Received 15 Horses & 3 mules	
	23rd		Mounted Drill at 1.30 A.M. Foot Drill 2 p.m. Inspected Glanders R.E. 4113th	
			Machine Gun Section	
	24th		Stable Picquet Inspection at 2 p.m.	
	25th		Mounted Drill at 6 A.M. Inspected Ambulance Horse Transport. Relieve 2.30 p.m.	
	26th		Foot Drill 2 p.m. Inspected D.A.C. Detail by A.D.V.S.	
	27th		Evacuated 19 Horses & 15 Mules	
	28th		P.M. at BETHUNE 9.30 A.M.	
	29th		Medical Inspection 9 A.M. Inspected No 4 Sec. D.A.C. & No 3 Sec D.A.C.	
	30th		Inspection of Glanders R.E.	
	31st		Inspection of 145th Heavy Group R.E.	

June 1st 1916
Jean Manur Lt. Av.C.
b.e 49th Mobile Vet. Section

XXXVIII

S. Lunt
49. M.Vet.Sec
Vol 7

SECRET.

Confidential War Diary.
of
Lieut. P. Howard. A.V.C.
O.C.
49th Mobile Vet. Section.

(Volume VII)

From June 1st. to June 30th 1916.

WAR DIARY
or
INTELLIGENCE SUMMARY
(Erase heading not required.)

Army Form C.

Instructions regarding War Diaries and Intelligence Summaries are contained in F.S. Regs., Part II. and the Staff Manual respectively. Title Pages will be prepared in manuscript.

Place	Date	Hour	Summary of Events and Information	Remarks and references to Appendices
LA GORGUE	June 1st	5 p-	Mules dict at 6 A.M. Man went to Baths at 2 p.m. Inspected First Army Ann. Area to Inspected Man riflu. Walis D.A. & Details	
	" 2nd		Returns the last Chankts. fm Park Man. Hones Foot Drill at 2-15 p.m.	
	" 3rd		Church Parade at 9-15 A.m.	
	" 4th		Inspected Horses Saddling	
	" 5th		Evacuate 13 Horses + 2 Mules	
	" 6th		My G.S. Animes From Repairs	
	" 7th		Read out on Parade Special Order of the Day Re P. M.s Kitchener Death. Foot Drill 2 p.m.	
	" 8th		Foot Drill 4 P.m Mounted Drill 6 A.M. Inference A.D.V.S Office.	
	" 9th		Evacuate 21 horses at 2 p.m.	
	" 10th		Church Parade 9-15 A.M.	
	" 11th		Evacuate 31 Horses + 2 Mules	
	" 12th		Lt LA GORGUE at 9-15 AM arrives in billets at BUSNES 3 p.m	
BUSNES	" 13th		Issued kit Horses arrives Daylight Saving inden at 11 p m	
	" 14th		Lft BUSNES at 12 Noon arrives AVEHEL 5.30. p.m	
AVEHEL	" 15th		Lft AVEHEL 9-30 A.m arrives St MICHEL at 5. p.m. Billets here very filthy	
St MICHEL	" 16th		issued men with Sheep wh'cjse.	
	" 17th		Evacuate 2 Horses Inspected Shires of 37th M.V.S. They appears in bad state	

WAR DIARY or INTELLIGENCE SUMMARY

Army Form C. 2118

Place	Date	Hour	Summary of Events and Information	Remarks and references to Appendices
St MICHEL	June 18th	5 pm	Rifle Inspection at 12 Noon. Pages Mess at 5-30 pm	
	19th	5 pm	Monks Call at 6 AM. Report PANTER & INTERPRETER prev to BUSNES P. Sick hunt.	
	20th	6 pm	Report PANTER returns with horse & float at 5-30 pm	
	21st	6 am	Guards 16 Sick Horses	
	22nd	5 pm	Foot inspection at 9-30 AM Pte PEARCE arrives from Hospital	
	23rd	5 pm	Guards 13 Sick Horses	
	24th		Rifle inspection at 12 Noon	
	25th		Guards parade at 6-15 AM. Left St MICHEL 6 pm Arrived BOFFLES	
	26th		Guards 16 Horses & 1 Mule Left St MICHEL 6 pm Arrived BOFFLES	
BOFFLES	27th		at 2 AM. Gun Retirn Inspection at 9 AM.	
LANCHES	27th		Left BOFFLES at 9.25 pm Arrived LANCHES 3-30 AM. Rifle inspection at 4-30 pm	
	28th		Guards & Horses. Unit has not to move at 6 pm.	
	29th		Guards & Horses	
	30th		Left for 2 Float Cover at 4 AM Guards & Horses Unit left LANCHES at 5 pm	

Pay Attn to H.Q.
Panthers Motor Ave
July 5th 1916. O.C. 44th M.V.S.

SECRET

COFIDENTIAL WAR DIARY

of

LIEUT P. HOWARD. A.V.C.
O.C.
49ᵗʰ MOBILE VET. SECTION

(VOLUME VIII)

From July 1st 1916. to July 31st 1916.

ORIGINAL

Vol 8

WAR DIARY or INTELLIGENCE SUMMARY

Army Form C. 2118

Place	Date	Hour	Summary of Events and Information	Remarks and references to Appendices
SEPTONVILLE	July 1st	—	Arrived at SEPTONVILLE at 2 A.M. Standing by for further move at 6.30 P.M.	
	July 2nd		Arrived of 13 sick lines orders received awaiting move.	
			Left SEPTONVILLE in execution of orders of 11 hours at FRENCHENCOURT — The return moved at	
LEALVILLERS	July 3rd		8.30 A.M arrived at LEALVILLERS at 2 P.M.	
			Evacuated if 14 hours at ACHEUX. Lt. LEALVILLERS at 10 P.M.	
TREUX	July 4 5	8 pm	Arrived at TREUX at 4 A.M. Evacuated 12 hours at MERICOURT L'ABBÉ	
	July 5		Evacuated 2 hours	
	July 6		Rifle & Spur inspection at 9.30 A.M.	
	" 7	6	Left for A.D.V.S. at HORLANCOURT. Visits & site of outposts.	
	" 8	5	Engd Mr. 49th M.V.S. Evg & 4 hr horses to hospital New "Grove Town"	
	" 9		Evacuated 8 horses	
	" 10		Inspection of harness & saddlery at 10 A.M	
	" 11	5	Evacuated 8 horses & 1 mule.	
	" 12	8	Evacuated 5 horses & 1 mule. Left YREUX at 6.30 p.m.	
POISY	July 13th	5	Arrived POISY at 3 A.M. Left at 10 A.M.	
PONT RÉMY	July 14th		Arrived PONT RÉMY at 1 A.M.	
	15th		Left PONT RÉMY at 6 A.M. Marching all day.	
POUIN	" 16th		Arrived POUIN at 1 A.M. Both horses & the lines done. Moved to FAMECHON at 7 p.m.	
FAMECHON	" 17	—	Evacuated 11 horses & 1 mule at BELLE ÉGLISE	

WAR DIARY
or
INTELLIGENCE SUMMARY
(Erase heading not required.)

Army Form C. 2118

Place	Date	Hour	Summary of Events and Information	Remarks and references to Appendices
FAMECHON	18th	5 p-	Visits PANDAS & home left by 11½ Lt BSP	
	19th		Guards 9 hours & Mules Inspection & Small Equipment at 4-30 p.m.	
	20th		Men went to Baths at 3 p.m at LOUIN	
	21st		Guards of 18 hours & 1 mule. Conference at A.D.V.S at LOUIN	
	22nd		Lopsticks by DDVS Heavy Army at 1 p.m.	
	23rd		Guards of 38 hours & 1 mule.	
	24th		Rifle Inspect 9 A.M. Saddlery at 2-30 p.m. Main Pay at 6-30 p.m.	
	25th		Guards of 22 hours. Visits MILLY fm horse lft.	
			Visits LE SOUICH & LONGHY SUR CANCHE & horse left Mule letter place	
			have 30 km. fm. my Section	
	27th		Guards 42 hours & 1 Mule Visits DOULLENS & HEM & Lft. Lunn	
			Pp. TAMECHON 4 p. Cmgnies SARTON 5. 30. p.m. Maashus 13 Animals & 32 Mules	
	28th		A.D.V.S visit his lillet Guards 23 Remount horses.	
SARTON	29th		11 A.M. SARTON 11 A.H Arrives BEAUVAL 1-30 p.m.	
	30th		Lft BEAUVAL 4 A.M. Entrains CANDAS 11-6 A.M. Arrives St. OMER 5 p.m	
ESQUELBERG	31st		Arrives by M.T.S. ESQUELBERG 11-30 p.m.	
	During		the Month of Harry travelling Our only transport has been the horse Plight & me	
			Sunn's Waggon, in my Opinion there is Obviously small q Maws & Arec g. s	
			be 4 g MVC	

General Staff,
38th. Division.

Attached please find Original War Diary,
Volume IX. compiled by O.C. 49th. Mobile Vety.
Section, for month of AUGUST, 1916.
Please acknowledge.

                                        Major. A.V.C.
        A.D.V.S. 38th. (Welsh) Division.

1st. September 1916.

Original

Vol 9

SECRET

CONFIDENTIAL WAR DIARY

OF

CAPT. P. HOWARD A.V.C.

O.C. 49th MOBILE VET: SECTION

(VOLUME IX)

FROM AUGUST 1st 1916 to AUGUST 31st 1916.

WAR DIARY or INTELLIGENCE SUMMARY

Army Form C. 2118

Place	Date	Hour	Summary of Events and Information	Remarks and references to Appendices
ESQUELBECQ Staff.	Aug 1st	—	Inspection of B.S.U.E. by A.D.V.S.	
	2nd		Visits St LAURENT & ESQUELBECQ to select horses for Lollies for other div[isions]	
	3rd		Visits MILLIAN & VOLKERINCKHOVE to collect horses — Had Divisional's marching order parade at 2 pm	
	4th		Luncheon A.D.V.S. office	
	5th		Proceeds 3 horses to St OMER No 23rd Vet Hospital by vans	
	6th		Visits the WATOO - PIPPERINGHE road & lane	
	7th		Remount Holiday. Draft sent for repairs to 332 E. Ke	
	8th		Rifle Inspection at 2 pm	
	9th		Saddle inspection at 10-30 am Pages read at 6 pm	
	10th		Proceeds 11 horses to St OMER. Change billets & left ESQUELBECQ at 7-45pm arrived LEORINGHAM at 9-30 pm	
LEORINGHAM	11th		Luncheon at A.D.V.S. office Lupkils equipment at 2.0 pm	
	12th		Visits CASSEL to have lunch by the 19th D.A.C.	
	13th		Inspect & hire horses to STRAZEELE & horses took leave at 6 AM	
	14th		Quarter of horses attend to St OMER	
	15th		On Hunt drill at 2 pm	
	16th		Proceeds of 9 horses & 1 mule to St OMER — Allies to 130th F.A. & three suffering with Tetanus	
	17th		Visits F.A. at 1 am. & 4 AM + 7-30pm Am and alltogether 25 on with Ack T leave	
	18th		Pt[e]s EDWARDS & MASON went sick late M + D towards of horses to St OMER	

WAR DIARY or INTELLIGENCE SUMMARY

Army Form C. 2118

Place	Date	Hour	Summary of Events and Information	Remarks and references to Appendices
LEDRINGHEM	Aug 20th		Proceeds 4 horse + 1 mule collects 2 horses from ARNEKE - Gas helmet drill at 4-30 p.m.	
	21st		Left LEDRINGHEM at 9-15 A.M. Arrives WATOU 1 p.m. The 4th M.V.S. has at present with	
WATOU	22nd		Pte EDWARDS & Dr. EDWARDS. evacuates to Hospital 13th F.A.	
	23rd		Visits HERZEELE from his sick by 3/5 D.A.E.	
	24th		Pays men 9 A.M. Pte GOODWIN places in Guard room for Virtue & stealing a N.C.O. at 2-15 p.m.	
	25th		Visits HERZEELE & ZEGGERS CAPPEL for sick horses: Orders Pte WRIGHT to clean latrine etc -	
			Refuses at A.P.V.S. His enquiry & took down summary of evidence in case of Goodwin. Remarks	
	26th		Pte WRIGHT has been charged my order & placed in trenches upon arrival.	
			Gas Helmet inspection at 9-15 A.M. Pte GOODWIN Remarks for F.G.C.H. Pte WRIGHT	
	27th		Refuses to obey my order to accept my orders. Remarks for F.C.C.M.	
	28th		4th M.V.S. leaves my billet 4th M.V.S. take over.	
	29th		Visits 112th F.A.	
			Guards of L. Horses to St. OMER via RYVELD, 1st Day ZUYTPEENE 2nd day. St. OMER	
	30th		3rd Day	
	31st		Dr. EDWARDS & Pte EDWARDS return from Hospital	

Geo Harris Capt A.V.C.
be 4th M.V.S.
31-8-16

Vol 10

Original

SECRET

CONFIDENTIAL WAR DIARY

OF

CAPT: P. HOWARD A.V.C.

49ᵗʰ MOBILE VET: SECTION

(VOLUME X)

FROM SEPT: 1ˢᵗ 1916 TO SEPT 30ᵗʰ 1916.

WAR DIARY
or
INTELLIGENCE SUMMARY

Army Form C. 2118.

Place	Date	Hour	Summary of Events and Information	Remarks and references to Appendices
WATOU	1st		L.&E.M. of 1 Pte Goodwin at POPERINGHE 10.9 am.	
	2nd		Rifle instruction at 9.15 am. Gas helmet inspection	
	3rd		Sgt proceeds to Gas school for instruction at 10.30 am.	
	4th		Three horses destroyed, sentence of C. in C. Goodwin promulgated, 2 yrs H. Labour	
	5th		Evacuation of thirty four horses & two mules to St Omer. The YALLOP reports for duty	
	6th		L.&E.M. of 1 Pte WRIGHT at Camp D. 114th Infantry Bde.	
	7th		Six horses received from 3rd Canadian Mobile Vet. Section	
	8th		Seven men of M.C.O.'s returning from ST OMER. Attend Conference at A.D.V.S. Office.	
	9th		Pte WRIGHT's sentence promulgated, 28 days F.P. No 1.	
	10th		Men paraded at 4.30. P.M.	
	11th		Rifle inspection 2.0 p.m. Saddle inspection 2.30 p.m.	
	12th		Evacuation of 145 horses & 2 mules, Sgts DICE & POLKINGHORNE proceed to No 2 Vet Hosp/P.	
	13th		Remittal of 1 Pte GOODWIN to prison.	
	14th		Collection of two horses left by 3rd Canadian Division	
	15th		Conference at ADVS. 19 horses arrive from D.A.C. Sgt CAMPBELL transferred to 113th Infantry Bde.	

Army Form C. 2118.

WAR DIARY
INTELLIGENCE SUMMARY.
(Erase heading not required.)

Instructions regarding War Diaries and Intelligence Summaries are contained in F. S. Regs., Part II. and the Staff Manual respectively. Title pages will be prepared in manuscript.

Place	Date	Hour	Summary of Events and Information	Remarks and references to Appendices
WATOU	Sept 16th		Pte's HORNE & LIVINGSTONE for medical inspection from No H.M.V.S. Gen admit inspection. Cpl PANTER proceeds to NEUFCHATEL	
	"17th"		Host came to D.A.C. Special Range came from 4th DIVISION (Parasote forme)	
	"18th"		Visit to C.R.E. Adjutant at 9.0 a.m. Cpl PANTER returned from NEUFCHATEL	
	"19th"		Evacuation of 51 horses & 4 mules to ST OMER	
	"20th"		Hort case to be at WIPPENHOEK by 6.0 a.m.	
	"21st"		Received strong mule from 13th Welsh Regt	
	"22nd"		Received strong horse from South Midland Hy. Bty. Conference at A.D.V.S.	
	"23rd"		Got new actisem from S+ OMER. Staff Capt's chargers returned to field Remount Section 2nd Army	
	Sept 24th		Gas Adm inspection 9.0 a.m., Rifle inspection	
	"24th"		Rifle inspection at 9.0 a.m., Kit inspection at 10.0 a.m. Pte CARR reports for duty, shot & buried a horse with broken leg at 6 p.m.	
	"25th"		Horse inspection at 10.30 a.m.	
	"26"		14 horses & 2 mules evacuated from WIPPENHOCK & 14 horses evacuated by road to ST OMER	

WAR DIARY
~~INTELLIGENCE SUMMARY~~
(Erase heading not required.)

Army Form C. 2118.

Place	Date	Hour	Summary of Events and Information	Remarks and references to Appendices
WATOU	Sept 27th		1 horse & 1 mule discharged to H.Q.'rs	
	" 28		A.D.V.S. proceeds on leave, taken over duties of A.D.V.S. by Lt & manipulation from NEUFCHATEL	
	" 29		Conference at A.D.V.S.	
	" 30		Attend D.D.V.S. Conference. Pte Cook reports for duty, received two horses found straying, from 19th Batt Welsh pioneers.	

Per Amos Capt A.V.
C.C. 48 M.V.S.

[Stamp: 48th MOBILE VETERINARY SECTION 1-10-16]

Vol II

General.

Confidential War Diary.

of.

Capt. P. Howard. A.V.C.

49th Mobile Vet. Section.

(Volume XI)

From Oct. 1st. to 8 Oct. 31st 1916.

Army Form C. 2118.

WAR DIARY
or
INTELLIGENCE SUMMARY.
(Erase heading not required.)

Instructions regarding War Diaries and Intelligence Summaries are contained in F. S. Regs., Part II. and the Staff Manual respectively. Title pages will be prepared in manuscript.

Place	Date	Hour	Summary of Events and Information	Remarks and references to Appendices
WATOU	Oct 1st 1915		Daylight saving time alters at 1 A.M.	
	2nd		A Sticky mud. Went to see Army Field Remount Section.	
	3rd		Inspection of 20 horses & three mules	
	4th		Visits 13th Fd Ambulance	
	5th		Rifle Inspection	
	6th		Conference at ADVS office	
	7th		Sick Horses inspected. Relieves sick horses from the 19th Division	
	8th		Relieves 1 horse from 19th Div. ADVS Returns from Loos	
	9th		Major Horne Ret. to Army Remount Section. Relieves 14 mules & one from 332 C. M.C.	
	10th		Evacuates of 21 horses & 2 mules	
	11th		Visits 180 Fd Ambulance	
	12th		Relieves 5 horses & influenza for treatment.	
	13th		One horse evacuates by road in special horse train. Inspects 4 OOR Lens	
	14th		Army & horse to control. Mess pres. KITCHENER &was	
	15th		Sick Horses inspected. Pd. Ch. to Fd. Amb. KITCHENER too. Relieves great horse visit. Raph 63 horse Wide Ship. Exchanges half a horse.	

Army Form C. 2118.

WAR DIARY
or
INTELLIGENCE SUMMARY.
(Erase heading not required.)

Place	Date	Hour	Summary of Events and Information	Remarks and references to Appendices
WATOU	Oct 16		Visits to Reg. School & intake in Latrine. Utilized Remmy.	
	17th		44 Horses & 6 Mules evacuated to No. 2 V.H.	
	18th		2 Horses Sickness. Bus to 11th Res⁴?	
	19th		Pte HORNE & LIVINGSTONE Ave. Knocker to Bligh. WATCH	
	20th		Influenza at hos⁹. Pte. HILL & MARSHALL admit hosp. Syly.	
	21st		Gas & Shell Helmet Inspection – also Rifle Inspection. Men Bathed at 2.30 pm	
	22nd		Pack Mule died at 6-30 AM.	
	23rd		Sylvian 156 Horses & Svatili all from 30ᵗʰ Div.	
	24th		Brigade of 188 & Horses & Mules to 23ʳᵈ V.H. Three horses drowned in Punt. Then were	
			active here.	
	25th		Nights. No. 3 Sec. three Hall	
	26th		Influenza at A.D.V.S. Officer that attend from bidunce pass him at 6 pm	
	27th		Visits three litt Cyclists glasses of 14th R.E. & 14th Pt. NAYLOR w.	
			admitted to hospital with Syph from d Reg⁴	
	28th		Spland. SMITH. Admitted to hospital held Brielt	
			Evacuates 32 Horse to St OMER Steam & Mini use clothing	
	29th		Part Norres Capt Ave	
	30ᵗʰ		1-11-16 6 & 49ᵗʰ M.V.S.	

Original

Vol 12

CONFIDENTIAL WAR DIARY.
of
Capt. P. Howard. A.V.C.
4/9th MOBILE VET. SECTION

Volume XII

From Nov. 1st 1916. to Nov. 30th 1916.

WAR DIARY or INTELLIGENCE SUMMARY.

(Erase heading not required.)

Army Form C. 2118.

Place	Date	Hour	Summary of Events and Information	Remarks and references to Appendices
WATOU	Nov 1st		Two Horses Strayed claimed by Belgian Army	
	" 2nd		1 Mule evac by rail to 13 USA Hospital. C.L. 41 & 4th U.S. Gr Train	
	" 3rd		C.L. returned	
	" 4th		Lee Helmet Inspection from NEUFCHATEL	
	" 5th		Pt Maybee Discharged from Hospital Ret'd 2.30 p.m.	
	" 6th		M Shoeing Insp. to C.O.Y.	
	" 7th		Herses L/S H.9 V.S. M. L 63 J.85 Ret'd. Two short Peres	
	" 8th		Conf of 20 Horses + 4 Mules	
	" 9th		Foot Drill 1-30 p.m.	
	" 10th		Rifle Drill 6-30 a.m.	
	" 11th		Conference at D.V.G	
	" 12th		Gas Helmet Inspection 9-0 a.m. Pte Hardie reports for Duty	
	" 13th		Evac of 3 Horses + 5 Mules by Rail. Bn. Replenishes Latrines at 2p.m.	
	" 14th		Inspection of Gas Helmets, Rifles, & ammunition 9-0 a.m.	
	" 15th		Sgt Brooks proceeds on Leave Eve of 26 Horses	
	" 16th		Inspection Mk saddlery at 11 a.m. L/Cpl Smith returns from Hospital	

WAR DIARY
or
INTELLIGENCE SUMMARY.
(Erase heading not required.)

Army Form C. 2118.

Place	Date	Hour	Summary of Events and Information	Remarks and references to Appendices
WATOU	Nov 17		Left & others returned from ST. OMER.	
	18		Lve Abbott & Riff Inspection 9-0 a.m. Lith 2.30 p.m.	
	19		Escd. of 5 Horses by Rail.	
	20		J. L. Hughes proceeds on Leave	
	21		Escd. of 25 Horses to ST. OMER.	
	22		Foot Drill 8.30 a.m. M/U drill 2.0 p.m.	
	23		Lieut Hobart Lefevre 2 p.m.	
	24		Conference A.G.V.S.	
	25		Lve Abbott, Supington & Riff Inspection 9.0 a.m. Lve Abbott proceeds on Leave. Minor Toys 6.0 p.m.	
	26		Horse Inspection 10-30 a.m.	
	27		Inspection of Harness & Saddlery 11-15 a.m.	
	28		Lt Chaput went off Leave. Escd of 22 Horses + 2 Mules	
	29		Lieut B 1917 and on. Co. 2-30 p.m.	
	30		Conference A.D.V.S.	

30-11-16.

Lieu-Anne S. Capt. A.V.C.
O.C. 49th Mobile Vet-Sech

Vet 13

Original

CONFIDENTIAL WAR DIARY

OF

P. HOWARD. CAPT. A.V.C

49th MOBILE VETERINARY SECTION

VOLUME XIII

From Dec: 1st 1916
To Dec: 31st 1916.

Army Form C. 2118.

WAR DIARY
or
INTELLIGENCE SUMMARY
(Erase heading not required.)

Instructions regarding War Diaries and Intelligence Summaries are contained in F.S. Regs., Part II. and the Staff Manual respectively. Title pages will be prepared in manuscript.

Place	Date	Hour	Summary of Events and Information	Remarks and references to Appendices
WATOU	Dec. 1st		Visit to 130th Field Ambulance, & 38th Div: Sig. Co.	
do	" 2nd	1.45 p.m.	Foot drill at 1.45 p.m.	
do	" 3rd	8.45 a.m.	S.S. Hughes returned from leave. Hoat Returned from Ordnance.	
do	" 4th		Drill with Box Respirator at 8.45 a.m.	
do	" 5th		Evacuation of 22 horses & 2 mules to No. 23rd Vet Hospital	
do	" 6th		Hoat crew at 12.2 Bde R.F.A., Visit to Div. Signal Co	
do	" 7th	3.0 p.m.	Attend conference at A.D.V.S. office at 3.0 p.m. Visit to Ledringhem.	
do	" 8th	9.0 a.m.	Sgt Harris returned from leave, Pte Royton Returned from A.D.V.S.	
do	" 9th	9.0 a.m.	Inspection of Rifles, P.H. helmets, & Box respirators at 9.0 a.m.	
do	" 10th	6.0 p.m.	Rifle Drill at 6.0 p.m. Gun's Roy at 6.0 p.m.	
do	" 11th	7.30 a.m.	Two men proceed to Ledringhem at 7.30 a.m.	
do	" 12th	7.30 a.m.	Three Hoat cases at 7.30 a.m. Evacuation of 14 horses.	
do	" 13th		Evacuation of 3 horses & 1 mule by mil. Officer i/c of sick home train	
do	" 14th		O.C. Returns from Evacuation	
do	" 15th	9.30 a.m.	The horse A Ponies on 2nd, Shores from WATOU at 9.30 a.m. arrived at LEDRINGHEM at 12.30 p.m.	

Army Form C. 2118.

WAR DIARY
or
INTELLIGENCE SUMMARY.
(Erase heading not required.)

Instructions regarding War Diaries and Intelligence Summaries are contained in F. S. Regs., Part II. and the Staff Manual respectively. Title pages will be prepared in manuscript.

Place	Date	Hour	Summary of Events and Information	Remarks and references to Appendices
LEDRINGHEM	Dec. 16th		Cpl. Parker & Pte. Cook return from leave.	
do	" 17th		Pte. Waite proceeds to Watou, O.C. takes over units in H.Q. Qrm. Area.	
do	" 18th		Talk over branches to be followed in at Lederingham	
do	" 19th		O.C. visits ARNEKE to collect home left behind by 39th Division	
do	" 20th		Evacuation of 16 horses & 1 mule to No 23 Vety. hospital. Sgt. Mummerby & Pte. Bowen arrive at 6.30 p.m.	
do	" 21st		Sgt. Hart & L/Cpl. Smith left for CAESTRE and returned. Pte. Smith proceeds on leave.	
do	" 22nd		Sgt. Hart & L/Cpl. Smith proceed to St. Omer en route for FORGES LES EAUX. Sgt. Campbell's team cancelled	
do	" 23rd		Inspection of Rifles, Steel helmets, P.H. helmets & Box Respirators at 9.0 am	
do	" 24th		Evacuation of 24 horses & 1 mule to No 23 Vety. Hospital	
do	" 25th		Christmas Day. The section have a very good time.	
do	" 26th		Visit to MERCKEGHEM for horse left by R.E.	
do	" 27th		Sgt. Mummerby proceeds to relieve Sgt. Campbell 113th M. Inft. Bde, Pte. Gallop proceeds on leave.	
do	" 28th		Visit to units of 113 Infantry Bde.	

WAR DIARY
or
INTELLIGENCE SUMMARY.
(Erase heading not required.)

Army Form C. 2118.

Instructions regarding War Diaries and Intelligence Summaries are contained in F. S. Regs., Part II. and the Staff Manual respectively. Title pages will be prepared in manuscript.

Place	Date	Hour	Summary of Events and Information	Remarks and references to Appendices
LEBRINGHEM	Dec 29	9.30 AM	Attend Conference at A.D.V.S. office. Visit 124 Field Co R.E. Had ser 16th Bn R.W.F. Remounts. Inspection of Rifles, P.H. Helmets & Box Respirators at 9.0 am. Evacuation of 7 horses to No 23 Veterinary Hospital. Visit A.D.V.S. Division	(7.27 am)
do	11.00		Saddle inspection at 11.0 a.m.	

49th MOBILE VETERINARY SECTION.

Vol/14

Original

CONFIDENTIAL WAR DIARY

of

P. Howard. Capt. A.V.C.

49th MOBILE VET. SECTION

Volume XIV

From Jan 1st 1917.

To Jan 31st 1917.

Army Form C. 2118.

WAR DIARY
or
INTELLIGENCE SUMMARY.
(Erase heading not required.)

Instructions regarding War Diaries and Intelligence Summaries are contained in F. S. Regs. Part II. and the Staff Manual respectively. Title pages will be prepared in manuscript.

Place	Date	Hour	Summary of Events and Information	Remarks and references to Appendices
LEDRINGHEM	Jan 1st 1917		PTE. MASON proceeds on leave. 49th M.V.S. granted 420 hams from Divisional canteen funds.	
"	2"		PTE SMITH returned off leave	
"	3rd		Visit to NORDAUSQUES for horse Left by 121st Brigade R.F.A.	
"	4th		Foot drill at 2·15 p.m., Box Respirator Drill at 2·45 p.m.	
"	5th		Visit to EPERLECQUES for horse Left by 119th Brigade R.F.A.	
"	6th		Inspection of Box Respirators and P.H. helmets at 9.0 a.m., PTE ACRES proceeds on leave.	
"	7th		Men paid at 4.0 p.m.	
"	8th		PTE BREWSTER reported sick.	
"	9th		PTE YALLOP returned off leave	
"	10th		A.D.V.S. Proceeds on leave. Visit A.D.V.S. Office and took over A.D.V.S. duties, Generals have arrived for Evacuation	
"	11th		PTE. BOND proceeds on leave.	
"	12th		One Sergeant and one man inoculated.	
"	13th		Evacuation of six horses to ST OMER at 8·45 a.m. Inspection of Box Respirators and P.H helmets.	
"	14th		PTE. MASON Returned off leave.	
"	15th		Rifle inspection at 9.0 a.m. Two float cases received from No 4. Section D.A.C., Visit A.D.V.S. Office.	

Army Form C. 2118.

WAR DIARY
or
INTELLIGENCE SUMMARY.
(Erase heading not required.)

Instructions regarding War Diaries and Intelligence Summaries are contained in F.S. Regs., Part II and the Staff Manual respectively. Title pages will be prepared in manuscript.

Place	Date	Hour	Summary of Events and Information	Remarks and references to Appendices
LEDRINGHEM	Jan 16th 1917		PTE PEARCE proceeds on leave. Evacuation of NINE horses to ST OMER	
"	" 17th		Attended D.D.V.S. Conference on behalf of A.D.V.S. Evacuation of TEN horses and TWO mules to ST OMER.	
"	" 18th		PTE ACRES returned off leave. Sgt & TWO men arrive from 1/1 WEST LANCASHIRE M.V.S. to take over billet.	
"			TWO mules destroyed. Visit A.D.V.S. Office.	
"	" 19th		Left LEDRINGHEM at 9.15 a.m. arrive at WATOU at 2.15 midday	
WATOU	" 20th		PTE MASON reported sick, hun paid at 7.30 pm visit A.D.V.S. Office	
"	" 21st		Cpl STRICKLAND proceeds on leave. PTE MASON admitted to hospital	
"	" 22nd		A.D.V.S. returned off leave. Sgt LONES reports for duty	
"	" 23rd		Evacuation of EIGHTEEN horses to ST OMER	
"	" 24th		PTE BOND returned off leave. PTE COOK admitted into hospital	
"	" 25th		Horse procession for horses of 104 Bde "A" Column but the horse had been moved	
"	" 26th		Attended Conference at A.D.V.S. Office. Foot drill at 2.0 pm.	
"	" 27th		Inspection of Box Respirators, P.H. helmets and Rifles	
"	" 28th		Saddle inspection at 11.0 a.m. ONE horse destroyed belonging to "C" 121 Bde. R.F.A.	
"	" 29th		Received THREE horses from 21st Division. ONE mule destroyed belonging to No 1. Sec. D.A.C., ONE horse destroyed belonging to "C" 121 Bde. R.F.A.	

Army Form C. 2118.

WAR DIARY
or
INTELLIGENCE SUMMARY.
(Erase heading not required.)

Instructions regarding War Diaries and Intelligence Summaries are contained in F. S. Regs., Part II. and the Staff Manual respectively. Title pages will be prepared in manuscript.

Place	Date	Hour	Summary of Events and Information	Remarks and references to Appendices
WATOU	Jan 30th		Evacuation of horses cancelled, ONE horse destroyed belonging to "C" Batty 12, Bde R.F.A.	
"	" 31st		Inspection of horses of Signal Co, visit to A.D.V.S. Office, ONE horse destroyed belonging "C" 94 Bde R.F.A. 31st Div.	

Paris Armas. Capt A.V.C.
O.C. 49th Mob. Vet. Section.

[Stamp: 49th MOBILE VETERINARY SECTION. No. ..... Date 1-2-17]

Vol/5

CONFIDENTIAL WAR DIARY

of

P. HOWARD. CAPT. A.V.C.

49th MOBILE VET. SECTION

VOLUME XV

ORIGINAL

From Feb. 1st 1917.
to Feb. 28th 1917

Army Form C. 2118

WAR DIARY
or
INTELLIGENCE SUMMARY.
(Erase heading not required.)

Instructions regarding War Diaries and Intelligence Summaries are contained in F. S. Regs., Part II. and the Staff Manual respectively. Title pages will be prepared in manuscript.

Place	Date	Hour	Summary of Events and Information	Remarks and references to Appendices
WATOU	Feb. 1st 1917		PTE PEARCE returned off Leave. Visit to Signal Co. (Home Lines)	
"	" 2nd		Attend conference at A.D.V.S. office, PTE WOODS reports for duty	
"	" 3rd		Inspection of P.H. Helmets & Box Respirators, 9.0 a.m. CPL STICKLAND Returned off Leave.	
"	" 4th		Respirator Drill at 9.0 a.m.	
"	" 5th		PTE WRIGHT Reported sick, Inspected Horses of Divisional Signal Co.	
"	" 6th		Sick animals not to be Evacuated (Roads closed)	
"	" 7th		Foot drill 9.0 a.m., Saddle and harness inspection at 11.0 a.m.	
"	" 8th		Visit Signal Co. (Home Lines)	
"	" 9th		Four horses shot, Attend Conference at A.D.V.S. office	
"	" 10th		Inspection of P.H. Helmets, Box Respirators, & Rifles at 9.0 a.m.	
"	" 11th		Received EIGHT horses suffering from STOMATITIS from 21st Division (for treatment)	
"	" 12th		PTE MASON Returned from hospital	
"	" 13th		Evacuation of 30 horses to ST. OMER	
"	" 14th		Received 3 horses from 34th Division	
"	" 15th		Attend Lecture on MANGE at No. 23 Vet. Hospital (ST. OMER), Inspected Horses of Signal Co.	
"	" 16th		Attend Conference at A.D.V.S. Office, Horse destroyed at No. 1 Sick Horse Lines	

Army Form C. 2118.

WAR DIARY
or
INTELLIGENCE SUMMARY.
(Erase heading not required.)

Place	Date	Hour	Summary of Events and Information	Remarks and references to Appendices
WATOU	Feb 17th 1917		Inspection of P.H. Animals, Box Respiratory & Rifles at 9.0 am. Sgt JONES Proceeded to No.2 Vet Hospital	
"	" 18th		Inspected Animals feet at 8.45 am, Foot & Rifle drill at 2.0 pm.	
"	" 19th		Sgt EDWARDS admitted to hospital	
"	" 20th		Evacuation of 31 Horses & 4 mules to ST. OMER	
"	" 21st		TWO (Surplus) Removed	
"	" 22nd		Received CHAFF CUTTER on loan, Inspected horses of Divisional Signal Co.	
"	" 23rd		Attend conference at A.D.V.S. Office, Buried TWO dead horses at No. 3. Sick horse Stables	
"	" 24th		Inspection of P.H. Animals, Box Respirators and Rifles at 9.0 am	
"	" 25th		Received 4,000 bricks for horse standings	
"	" 26th		Destroyed horse belonging to 21st Division, ONE Buen Inoculated	
"	" 27th		Evacuation of 32 Horses & 1 Mule to ST. OMER	
"	" 28th		Visit Second Army Purchasing Board for purpose of inspecting horses in "E" AREA	
"			Visit Signal Co. (Horse lines), Received 4,000 bricks for horse standings	

R. M. Evans. Capt. A.V.C.
O.C. 49th M.V.S.

40th MOBILE VETERINARY SECTION.
No. 674/17
Date 1-3-17

Vol-16

From March 1st 1917
To March 31st 1917

CONFIDENTIAL WAR DIARY

OF

P. HOWARD. CAPT. A.V.C.

No. 49 MOBILE VET. SECTION

VOLUME XVI

ORIGINAL

Army Form C. 2118.

WAR DIARY
or
INTELLIGENCE SUMMARY
(Erase heading not required.)

Instructions regarding War Diaries and Intelligence Summaries are contained in F. S. Regs., Part II. and the Staff Manual respectively. Title pages will be prepared in manuscript.

Place	Date	Hour	Summary of Events and Information	Remarks and references to Appendices
WATOU	January 1st		At Dawoo Loy, Reveille at 6.0 am	
"	2nd		Conference at A.D.V.S. Office, Visit to Signal Co's Horse Lines, 4 horses resound, one horse Distroyed	
"	3rd		Men's Pay at 6.0 pm.	
"	4th		Inspection of P.H. Helmets, Box Respirators and Rifles at 9.0 am	
"	5th		Issue of Quiet time to units of the Division	
"			Ranchos MARSHALL & YALLOP Report sick	
"	6th		Evacuated 31 horses & 1 mule to No. 23 Veterinary Hospital, Tested all P.H. Helmets & Box Respirators in possession of R.E.O's & Men through Gas Chamber	
"	7th		Two horses evacuated (Mange) discharged. Inspection of Horses at Signal Co.	
"	8th		Stray Horse dispatched to Army Remount Section	
"	9th		Received Mison Hut, Conference at A.D.V.S. Office, Visit to Signal Co.	
"	10th		Inspection of P.H. Helmets, Box Respirators & Rifles at 9.0 am.	
"	11th		Stray Horse received from 16th Bn Welsh Regt.	
"	12th		PTE BREWSTER Reports sick	
"	13th		Evacuated 38 horses & 7 mules to No. 23 Veterinary Hospital	
"	14th		Gunner EDWARDS Reports sick, Inspect Horses at Signal Co.	

Army Form C. 2118.

WAR DIARY
or
INTELLIGENCE SUMMARY

(Erase heading not required.)

Instructions regarding War Diaries and Intelligence Summaries are contained in F.S. Regs., Part II and the Staff Manual respectively. Title pages will be prepared in manuscript.

Place	Date	Hour	Summary of Events and Information	Remarks and references to Appendices
WATOU	March 15th		Horst Broke down at POPERINGHE	
"	" 16th		Conference at A.D.V.S. Office, CAPTAIN T.FINCH. A.V.C. arrives to take over Section 2nd Cavt. Signal Co.	
"	" 17th		Inspection of P.H. Schmels, Bod Respirators & Rifles at 9.0 am	
"	" 18th		Captain HOWARD. A.V.C. proceeds on Leave at 5.15 am.	
"	" 19th		Then took over NISSEN Hut. No Orders to horses to be received until further orders.	
"	" 20th		Evacuation of 14 horses + 1 Mule. To No. 23 Veterinary Hospital.	
"	" 21st		Two Horse Cases received from 332 Co. A.S.C. Inspect horses at Signal Co.	
"	" 22nd		Horse Received from C"Batty 122 Bde R.F.A	
"	" 23rd		Conference at A.D.V.S. Office, CPL. STICKLAND promoted SGT. dated 25/2/17, 2nd Cavt. Signal Co.	
"	" 24th		Inspection of Box Respirators & P.H. Schmels & Rifles at 9.0 am, 5 horses Returned	
"			to 21st DIVISION Convoy of "STOMATITIS CONTAGIOSA".	
"	" 25th		Clock time advanced 1 hour "Summer time", Visit to A.D.V.S.	
"	" 26th		SGT. STICKLAND A.V.C. proceeds to No.12 Veterinary Hospital for Duty.	
"	" 27th		Evacuation of 33 horses & 4 mules to No. 23 Veterinary Hospital	
"	" 28th		Horse Case Received from 332 Co. A.S.C., Inspection of horses at Signal Co.	
"	" 29th		Two horses Destroyed	

Army Form C. 2118.

WAR DIARY
or
INTELLIGENCE SUMMARY
(Erase heading not required.)

Instructions regarding War Diaries and Intelligence Summaries are contained in F. S. Regs. Part II. and the Staff Manual respectively. Title pages will be prepared in manuscript.

Place	Date	Hour	Summary of Events and Information	Remarks and references to Appendices
WATOU	March 30th		Conference at A.D.V.S. Office. Visit to Signal Co.	
"	31st		Inspection of P.H. helmets, Box Respirators & Rifles at 9.0 am. Capt. HOWARD Returned off leave. Received 1 mule which dropped dead on WATOU - POPERINGHE Rd. Capt. FINCH left this section.	

Jas Anns. Capt A.V.C.
b.c. 49 to hrs.

1-4-17.

Vol 17

CONFIDENTIAL WAR DIARY

OF

P. HOWARD.   CAPT.   A.V.C.

No. 49 MOBILE VET. SECTION

VOLUME XVII

From April 1st
To April 30th 1917

WAR DIARY or INTELLIGENCE SUMMARY

Army Form C. 2118.

Place	Date	Hour	Summary of Events and Information	Remarks and references to Appendices
WATOU	APRIL 1st 1917		Saddle Inspection at 11 a.m.	
"	2nd		Inspection of all animals received for evacuation by A.D.V.S.	
"	3rd		Evacuation of 45 horses & 3 mules by train. Evacuation of 140 horses & 3 mules by road to No. 23 Veterinary Hospital	
"	4th		Received 2000 bricks for horse standings	
"	5th		One horse destroyed belonging to Lancashire Hy. Bty. R.G.A.	
"	6th		Conference at A.D.V.S. Office. Inspection of horses at 38th Division Signal Co.	
"	7th		Box Respirators and P.H. helmets at 9.0 a.m.	
"	8th		Easter Sunday. Kit inspection at 8.45 a.m.	
"	9th		Received float cars from No.1 Sec. 38th D.A.C.	
"	10th		Evacuation of 19 horses and 7 mules to No. 23 Veterinary Hospital	
"	11th		Visit to Head Quarters Signal Co.	
"	12th		O.C. called out to 34 Bty. 169 Bde. R.F.A. to examine sick horse, S.S. Hughes inoculated	
"	13th		Conference at A.D.V.S. office, Proven Copse at 6.0 p.m.	
"	14th		Inspection of Box Respirators, P.H. helmets & Rifles at 9.0 a.m. Gas Alarm put at 10.30 a.m.	
"	15th		Inspection by A.A. & Q.M.G. & D.A.Q.M.G. at 11.30 a.m. Sgt. MUNNULLY proceeds to Camp "J".	

Army Form C. 2118.

WAR DIARY
or
INTELLIGENCE SUMMARY.
(Erase heading not required.)

Instructions regarding War Diaries and Intelligence Summaries are contained in F. S. Regs., Part II. and the Staff Manual respectively. Title pages will be prepared in manuscript.

Place	Date	Summary of Events and Information	Remarks and references to Appendices
WATOU	APRIL 16th	Received 40 horses for Evacuation.	
"	17th	Evacuation of 33 horses and 7 mules to No 23 Veterinary Hospital.	
"	18th	Two horses destroyed. PTE. NAYLOR reported sick.	
"	19th	Received one Trench cart from 15th Bn. R.W.F. at 9.0 p.m.	
"	20th	Conference at A.D.V.S. Office. CPL. PANTER proceeds to Divisional Gas School. Sgt. MUNNULLY returns from "J" Camp.	
"	21st	Inspection of Bot. Respirators, P.H. Helmets, Brandeliers and ammunition at 9.0 a.m.	
"	22nd	A.D.V.S. visits this Section. Inspection of horses at Hq. Div. Signal Co.	
"	23rd	PTE. ACRES awarded 7 days C.C. for Neglect of duty.	
"	24th	Evacuation of 24 horses and two mules by Road to No 23 Veterinary Hospital	
"	25th	CPL. YALLOP promotion: P.A./CPL. from 23/3/17.	
"	26th	Visit to WORM HOUDT to inspect horses of 129 Field Ambulances. CPL. PANTER returns from Gas School.	
"	27th	Conference at A.D.V.S. Office. Army Pay at 6.0 p.m.	
"	28th	Inspection of Box Respirators, P.H. Helmets, Haversacks, Gas Drill at 1.30 p.m.	
"	29th	Foot drill 12.15 — mid-day. Visit to Hq. Div. Signal Co.	
"	30th	PTEs HARDIE and HILL Reported sick. Accident to PTE. BOND's knee. Accidental shooting.	P. Thomas Capt. A.V.C. O.C. 49 Fd A.S.S.

CONFIDENTIAL WAR DIARY Vol 18

OF

CAPTAIN P. HOWARD. A.V.C.

No 49 MOBILE VET. SECTION

VOLUME XVIII

From May 1st. 1917
To May 31st. 1917

49 Mob Vety See
501

WAR DIARY
or
INTELLIGENCE SUMMARY
(Erase heading not required.)

Army Form C. 2118.

Place	Date		Summary of Events and Information	Remarks and references to Appendices
WATOU	MAY	1st 1917	Evacuated 39 horses and one mule to No. 23 Vet. Hospital. Visit Hd Qr Signal Co.	
"	"	2nd	Visit Hd Qr Signal Co.	
"	"	3rd	SERGT. BROOKS, PTE. WOODS, PTE. MASON and PTE. ACRES proceed to join VIII Corps Mobile Vety Detachment.	
"	"	4th	PTE. WAITE admitted into hospital. Received one mule from D.H.Q. for treatment. Conference at A.D.V.S. Office. Visit Hd Qr Signal Co.	
"	"	5th	Inspection of P.H Helmets, Box Respirators, and Rifles at 9.0 am, Rifle Drill at 9.15 am. Bath Parade at 2.0 pm, Received float ease from 114th M. Gun Co.	
"	"	6th	Box Respirator Drill at 12.30 pm.	
"	"	7th	Foot Drill at 9.0 am, Received eight Horses incl R.	
"	"	8th	Evacuated ten horses to No. 23 Veterinary Hospital	
"	"	9th	Pte. WAITE discharged from hospital. Destroyed one horse of C/119 Bde R.F.A.	
"	"	10th	Received one horse for staying by 114th M. Gun Co.	
"	"	11th	Received one horse from C/102 Bde R.F.A. 23rd Div.	
"	"	12th	Inspection of P.H Helmets, Box Respirators, and Rifles at 9.0, Rifle Drill at 9.15, Bath Parade at 2.0 pm.	

Army Form C. 2118.

WAR DIARY
or
INTELLIGENCE SUMMARY
(Erase heading not required.)

Instructions regarding War Diaries and Intelligence Summaries are contained in F.S. Regs., Part II. and the Staff Manual respectively. Title pages will be prepared in manuscript.

Place	Date	Hour	Summary of Events and Information	Remarks and references to Appendices
WATOU	May 13th 17		Foot drill at 9.0 a.m. Box Respirator Drill at 12.30 p.m.	
"	14th		Rifle Drill at 9.0 a.m., Received eight Horses n.R.	
"	15th		Evacuated seven horses to No. 23 Veterinary Hospital. Received one Horse of 151 Field Co. R.E.	
"	16th		Received one horse from 18/122 Bde. R.F.A.	
"	17th		Received eleven Head Collars from 18/119 Bde A.F.A. and fourteen from 8/119 Bde. A.F.A., Received two Head ropes from 15th Bn. R.W.F. and one from 113 M. Gun Co. O.C. proceeds to WORMHOUDT. Received twenty eight head collars from C/119 Bde. A.F.A.	
"	18th		O.C. Proceeds to conference at A.D.V.S, stay horse claimed by unit of Belgian Army.	
"	19th		Respirator and P.H. Helmet and Rifle inspection at 9.0 a.m. Rifle drill at 9.30am Foot drill 12.30 p.m.	
"	20th		Foot drill at 9.0 a.m., Respirator drill at 12.30, Received floatcase from No. 2 Section 38th D.A.C., one horse destroyed belonging to 151 Field Co. R.E., Mice Removed from Carcase.	
"	21st		Received float case from No. 2 Section 38 M.D.A.C., Received six horses n.R.	
"	22nd		Evacuated four sick horses to No. 23 Veterinary Hospital, inspection of horses at 11.30 pm Saddle inspection at 3.30 p.m.	
"	23		Issued one Rider to H.Q. Signal Co., one Rider to 124 Field Co. R.E. & one to 129 Field Ambulance	

WAR DIARY
or
INTELLIGENCE SUMMARY.
(Erase heading not required.)

Army Form C. 2118.

Place	Date	Hour	Summary of Events and Information	Remarks and references to Appendices
WATOU	Aug 24th 1917		Issued one Riding Horse to 114th Bde. M. Gun. Co., Two horses returned to D/122 Bde R.F.A. Received Two horses from D/119 Bde A.F.A. and one from D/119 Bde A.F.A., issued a horse to D/121 Bde R.F.A., Dr EDWARDS proceeds on leave, Sgt SMITH reports for duty.	
"	25th 1917		O.C. proceeds to Conference at A.D.V.S. Office, SGT SMITH proceeds to take over VIII Corps Mobile Veterinary Detachment, STAFF SGT BROOKS returned to 49th M.V.S., received one horse for treatment from D.H.Q.	
"	26th 1917		Inspection of Box Respirators, P.H. Helmets, and Rifles at 9.0 am, Rifle Drill at 9.15am Foot drill at 9 am, Respirator Drill at 12.30 pm, Received two horses from 129 Field Ambulance for treatment, STAFF SGT. BROOK'S proceeds to No.23 Vet. Hospital for duty.	
"	27th 1917			
"	28th 1917		Foot drill at 9 am, Received four horses sick, Returned one horse to D/119 Bde A.F.A.	
"	29th "		Evacuated six horses and one mule to No.23 Kelly Hospital, horse inspection at 11.30 am, saddle inspection at 4.0 pm.	
"	30th "		Received two stray horses from H.Q. M. M. P.	
"	31st "		Handed over two stray horses to WESSEX HANTS R.G.A., Received one stray case, and one horse from Base from Base section 38th D.A.P.	

P. Hmws. Rept Ave
b.e 49th M.V.S
1-6-17

Vol 19

original

CONFIDENTIAL WAR DIARY

OF

CAPT. P. HOWARD. A.V.C.

No. 49 MOBILE VET'Y. SECTION

VOLUME XIX

From 1st June 1917 to June 30th 1917

Army Form C. 2118.

WAR DIARY
or
INTELLIGENCE SUMMARY.
(Erase heading not required.)

Instructions regarding War Diaries and Intelligence Summaries are contained in F. S. Regs., Part II. and the Staff Manual respectively. Title pages will be prepared in manuscript.

Place	Date	Hour	Summary of Events and Information	Remarks and references to Appendices
WATOU	June 1st/917		Saddle inspection at 11.30 am, horse inspection at 2.30 pm; CPL. PANTER returned from No. 23 Veterinary Hospital.	
"	2nd		Inspection of Rifles, P.H. Helmets & Box Respirators at 9.0 am, Rifle Drill at 9.5 am, Bath parade at 2.30 pm.	
"	3rd		Foot drill at 9.0 am, Respirator Drill at 12.30 noon.	
"	4th		Received six horses, sick. PTE. PEARCE proceeded on leave to England.	
"	5th		Evacuation of four horses sick to No. 23 Veterinary Hospital	
"	6th		Received one horse from 330 Co. A.S.C. for treatment, one from 130 Field Ambulance for treatment. Received float case from No. 2 Section 38th D.A.C.	
"	7th		Received float case from No. 1 Sec. 38th D.A.C., and one float case from No. 2 Section 38th D.A.C. Saddle inspection at 11.30 am, horses inspection at 2.30 pm. Received three float cases from No. 2 Sec. 38th D.A.C. and one from No. 1 Sec. 38th D.A.C.	
"	8th		Received one horse from 18/22 Bde R.F.A. and one horse from No. 2 Sec. 38th D.A.C. Collected one horse left behind by 277 Bde. R.F.A., one float case from C/123 Bde R.F.A., Mens Pay 6.30 pm	
"	9th		Inspection of Rifles, P.H. Helmets & Box Respirators at 9.0 am, Rifle Drill at 9.5 am. Received one horse from No. 1 Sec. 38th D.A.C. and one from 124 Field Co R.E.'s	
"	10		Collected one stray mule. Bath parade at 2.30 pm, foot drill at 12.30 noon.	

WAR DIARY or INTELLIGENCE SUMMARY

Army Form C. 2118.

Place	Date	Hour	Summary of Events and Information	Remarks and references to Appendices
WATOU	June 11th 1917	9 a.m.	Respirator Drill 9 a.m. Received one horse from 332 Co. A.S.C., four from 2nd Corps H.Q. and three from "C" 2/10 Yorks Dragoons	
"	" 12th	"	Evacuation of one sick horse to No. 23 Veterinary Hospital	
"	" 13th	"	Harness inspection at 12.30 noon. Saddle inspection at 2.30 pm. Bath parade at 3.30 pm.	
"	" 14th	"	CPL. PANTER, PTE. HILL and PTE. MARSHALL proceed to take over billets, two horses and Evacuated to No. 23 Veterinary Hospital by Motor Horse Ambulance	
"	" 15th	"	Horses old killed at 11.0 am. arrive at new billet at 2.30 pm. Evacuation of two horses by (motor) sick horse ambulance to No. 23 Veterinary Hospital. Received one horse from H.Q.m. 38th Division for treatment, CPL VALLOP returned from 23 Vety. Hosp.	
VOX/VRIE	" 16th	"	Inspection of Rifles, P.H. Helmets + Box Respirators at 9.0 am. Received eight horses sick.	
"	" 17th	"	Rifle drill 9.0 am. foot drill at 2.30 pm. Bath parade at 3.30 pm.	
"	" 18th	"	Received two horses sick	
"	" 19th	"	Evacuation of twelve horses to No. 23 Veterinary Hospital.	
"	" 20th	"	Harness inspection at 11.30 am., Saddle inspection at 2.30 pm. Received one horse from 2/171 Bde. R.F.A.	
"	" 21st	"	Kit inspection	

Army Form C. 2118.

WAR DIARY
or
INTELLIGENCE SUMMARY.
(Erase heading not required.)

Instructions regarding War Diaries and Intelligence Summaries are contained in F.S. Regs., Part II. and the Staff Manual respectively. Title pages will be prepared in manuscript.

Place	Date	Hour	Summary of Events and Information	Remarks and references to Appendices
VOX VRIE	June 22nd 1917		Received on loan from 144 Hy.DMy, R.G.A., CPL PANTER. Returned from No. 23 Veterinary Hospital	
"	23rd 1917		Inspection of 144 detachate, Box Respirators and Rifles at 9.0 am. Two horses Received, transference	
"			Two sick horses to Corps Artill. Veterinary Detachment.	
"	24th		Foot drill at 9.0 am, Box Respirator Drill at 12.30 a.m.	
"	25th		Received five horses sick.	
"	26th		Evacuated sixteen sick horses by train. Received 16 horses sick, sent 2 horses to H.Q.	
"	27th		Horse inspection at 12.30 a.m., and stables inspection at 2.30 pm. Received 4 horses sick, Received 37 horses from 330 Co. A.S.C., and 18 horses from No 2 Sec 38 M.D.A.C., issued one horse to 331 Co. A.S.C.	
"	28th		CPL YALLOP Returned from leave, No.18 Smith NCy section arrives to take over camp	
"	29th		Received one horse for treatment from 15th Bn R.W.F., Evacuated VOX VRIE at 8.30 am, arrive at CAESTRE at 4.0 pm.	
"	30th		Left CAESTRE at 8.30 am, arrive at FONTES at 4.30 pm.	

1-7-17.

Penstones Capt A.V.C.
O.C. 49th M.V.S.

CONFIDENTIAL WAR DIARY No 26

OF

Capt. P. HOWARD. A.V.C.

No. 49 Mobile Veterinary Section

VOLUME XX

From 1st July 1917
To July 31st 1917

WAR DIARY or INTELLIGENCE SUMMARY.

(Erase heading not required.)

Army Form C. 2118.

Place	Date	Hour	Summary of Events and Information	Remarks and references to Appendices
FONTES	July 1st 1917		Inspection of Respirators, Pt Helmets, & Rifles 9 a.m. Rifle drill 9-10 a.m. Respirator drill 12-30 pm	
"	2	"	Saddle inspection 11-30. House inspection 2-30 P.M. Returned one mule to 13th WSA Regt. Received one horse 30th DAC	
"	3	"	Received 1 mule from 176 M.G. Co. for treatment. Pte PEARCE awarded 28 days No. 1 Field Punishment, for "Absence without leave". Inspection of Horse Ties, & Field Dressings at 9-45 a.m.	
"	4	"	Inspection of Bandolier & Ammunition 9 a.m. Horse inspection 3-30 p.m. Received 1 Horse by fleet from 131st FA	
"	5	"	Batt parade 2.30 p.m.	
"	6	"	Received 1 horse from 2 Sect 57 DAC, & 4 horses from # Batt 124 Bde RFA 37th Div. Pays out 6. pm	
"	7	"	Rifle drill 9-10 a.m. Respirator drill 2-30 p.m	
"	8	"	Foot drill 9-a.m. Received 1 horse from 331 & ASC	
"	9	"	Received 1 horse from # 2 Signal Co. 1 horse from 131st FA by fleet, & 1 horse from A Batt 250 Bde 56th Div	
"	10	"	Evacuated 12 horses by train. Cpl PAINTER, & Pte ELLIOT in charge	
"	11	"	Inspection of Box Respirators & Pt Helmets. Received 1 Horse from 56th Div	
"	12	"	Received 4 horses from D Batt 307 AFA RFA 61st Div, & 1 horse from 241 BDe 10 HA 48th Div. Horse inspection 3-30	
"	13	"	Evacuated 13 horses by train. Cpl YALLOP in charge.	
"	14	"	Received 2 horses from Australian RFA, & 1 horse from Australian DAC. Inspection of Box Respirator, Pt Helmets, & Rifles.	

WAR DIARY or INTELLIGENCE SUMMARY

Army Form C. 2118.

Place	Date	Summary of Events and Information	Remarks and references to Appendices
FONTE	July 15th-17	Foot drill at 9.0 am, Rifle Drill at 12.30 p.m., Exercised four horses, sick, Received one horse, passed by M.N.P.	
"	16th	Proved from FONTE at 9.30 am, Arrived TANNAY at 2.30 P.M., Rifle Inspection 6.0 P.M.	
TANNAY	17th	Left TANNAY at 4.30 A.M., Arrived CAESTRE at 10.0 A.M., PTE Proseilin leave.	
CAESTRE	18th	Left CAESTRE at 9.15 A.M., arrived at EECKE at 10.30 A.M., saddle inspection 4.30 pm.	
EECKE	19th	Left EECKE 6.30 am, arrived at PROVEN 3.30 P.M., Rifle inspection at 6.30 P.M.	
PROVEN	20th	Inspection of horses at 11.0 am. PTE. BREWSTER Returns from 1's 1/c., Dr. ANTHONY Returned of Leave, Cpl YALLOP, CPL PANTER & PTE HILL Return from 1's 1/c., PTE BREWSTER Reports sick.	
PROVEN	21st	Left PROVEN 9.0 AM., Arrived at VOX VRIE 11.0 AM., MEN'S PAY at 6.30 P.M., Received 23 sick horses from No. 18. M.V.S & 8 from Indus. Received six sick horses from mob of 38th Divn.	
"	22nd	Inspection of P.H. helmets, Box Respirators, Jack Spurs, steel helmets & Rifles at 9.0 am. Transferred 12 horses to No. 18. M.V.S. Destroyed 1 mule of 29th Division (TETANUS) GAS ALERT at 12.30 A.M.	
"	23rd	Received 2 Foot cases, & 6 sick horses. (1 from 9th Air Com Railway Troops)	
"	24th	Thirteen sick animals evacuated to Corps Shoot. Very Detachment. (5 of 29th Divn.) admitted two sick horses.	
"	25th	Rifle Drill at 9.0 am, Received 2 Foot cases & sick horses, inspection by Lt. Col. Murray, A.V.C.	

WAR DIARY
or
INTELLIGENCE SUMMARY.
(Erase heading not required.)

Army Form C. 2118.

Place	Date	Hour	Summary of Events and Information	Remarks and references to Appendices
VOXVRIE	July 26th 1917		Evacuated 2 Heat cases, and six walking cases to Corps C.C.S. admitted 1 horse sick	
"	27th		Heat and 4 horses sick	
"			Hacked to Corps O.C.S 4 horses, admitted one horse 27/28/1905 3 horses from 330 Co. A.S.E., SGT MUNNULLY proceed to Civil Pontoon duty.	
"	28th		Hacked 3 horses to Corps C.C.S. & 1 walking case, Evacuated to No 23 Vety Hospital by Road 16 sick animals & 2 Chargers belonging to Capt WALL AVC., 2 animals Evacuated by Motor Ambulance to No 23 Vet Hospital, Admitted 9 sick animals, Sgt MUNNULLY proceed to advanced Wareningy Post., PTE.ELLIOTT. Proceeds on leave to SCOTLAND.	
"	29th		Inspection of PH Helmet, Box Respirator, Rifles & Steel Helmet.	
"	30th		PTE.LITTLE Proceeds on Leave to ENGLAND, SGT. MUNNULLY Proceed to advanced Post, PTE WHITE returns from leave, admitted 7 horses & 2 mules sick, Evacuate 8 sick animals	
"	31st		Admitted 8 sick horses & 7 sick mules, Evacuated 17 sick animals to Corps C.C.S.	

1-8-17

Paul Amos Capt A.V.C.
to Mr Vet Sectn

6 c 49

Vol 21

Confidential War Diary
of
Capt P Howard AVC

No. 49 Mobile Veterinary Section

Vol XXI

From Aug 1st 1917   To Aug 31st 1917

Army Form C. 2118.

WAR DIARY
or
INTELLIGENCE SUMMARY.
(Erase heading not required.)

Instructions regarding War Diaries and Intelligence Summaries are contained in F.S. Regs., Part II. and the Staff Manual respectively. Title pages will be prepared in manuscript.

Place	Date	Hour	Summary of Events and Information	Remarks and references to Appendices
VOX VRIE	Aug 1		13 Animals admitted, 3 for Treatment. 2 Died & 3 were destroyed. 7 evacuated to XII Corps B.B.S.	
"	2		11 Animals admitted & 7 evacuated to XII Corps B.B.S. 2 Greys belonging to General admitted for Treatment	
"	3		8 animals admitted & 14 evacuated to XII Corps B.B.S. Paid out at 6.15 p.m	
"	4		Inspection of Rifles equipment & gas helmets. 14 animals admitted, & 7 animals & 7 Riders evacuated to B.B.S.	
"	5		Admitted 21 animals, evacuated 20 to B.B.S. 1 died at admission post.	
"	6		Admitted Major Williams charger for treatment, & evacd 6 other animals. Moved off at 10.45 am. Arrived PROVEN 1.0 pm	
PROVEN	7		Admitted 3 animals & evacuated 11 to B.B.S.	
"	8		Rifle drill at 9 a.m. Evacuated 5 animals to B.B.S. & issued 1 Mule to D.H.2	
"	9		Admitted 2 horses & cast 1 horse for destruction	
"	10		Batt parade at 2.0 p.m. PTE WHITE reports from leave	
"	11		Corpl Fante to 8 men proceed to B.B.S. for temporary duty. Evacuated 3 horses to B.B.S. PTE LITTLE reports from leave	
"	12		PTE MARSHALL proceeds on leave to England. Admitted 3 animals & destroyed 1	
"	13		Sgt MANNILLY proceeds on leave to England. Admitted 3 animals & evacuated 5. CMLS dipped 5 men as contracting pair	to M.V.D
"	14		Evacuated 3 animals to B.B.S. & issued 1 charger to D.H.2 PTE BREWSTER returns from leave	
"	15		Admitted 1 horse & issued 1. Stay PTE HILL proceeds on leave to England	

WAR DIARY
or
INTELLIGENCE SUMMARY.

(Erase heading not required.)

Army Form C. 2118.

Place	Date	Hour	Summary of Events and Information	Remarks and references to Appendices
PROVEN	Aug 16		Admitted 2 horses. Pte Wright proceeds on leave to England. Inspection of Gas School N.b.O.S.	
" "	17		Admitted 3 horses & evacuated 6 to 6.6.S. 1 discharged card to 130th Field Ambulance	
" "	18		Cpl Jollye & 2 men proceed to Abeenl port with float. Pte Write proceeds to take over from outgoing	
" "	19		Left PROVEN at 9.30 am. arrived at VOX VRIE at 12.15 pm. 1 Mule (dead) & 1 Tetanus case taken over from 32 D M.V.S. Receiving 13 horses from Abeenl port	
VOX VRIE	20		Admitted 21 horses & evacuated 30 to 6.6.S	
" "	21		Admitted 31 animals & evacuated 12 to 6.6.S	
" "	22		Admitted 39 animals & evacuated 35 to 6.6.S	
" "	23		Admitted 13 animals & evacuated 24 to 6.6.S	
" "	24		Admitted 40 animals. XIV bgde 6.6.S closed for evacuation	
" "	25		Admitted 13 animals. Inspection of Rifles Gas helmets, & gas mask 9.0 a.m.	
" "	26		Admitted 12 animals & evacuated 42 to 6.6.S. Sgt Munnery & Pte Marshall report from leave	
" "	27		Admitted 45 animals & evacuated 33 to 6.6.S	
" "	28		Admitted 2 animals & evacuated 39 to 6.6.S	
" "	29		Admitted 40 animals & evacuated 35 to 6.6.S	
" "	30		Admitted 30 animals & evacuated 37 to 6.6.S. Pte Hill reports from leave	
" "	31		Admitted 14 animals & evacuated 12 to 6.6.S	

Vol 22

CONFIDENTIAL

WAR DIARY
OF

CAPT P HOWARD AVC

No 49 MOBILE VETERINARY SECTION

VOL XXII

from SEPT 1st 1917 To SEPT 30th 1917

Army Form C. 2118.

WAR DIARY
or
INTELLIGENCE SUMMARY.
(Erase heading not required.)

Instructions regarding War Diaries and Intelligence Summaries are contained in F.S. Regs., Part II and the Staff Manual respectively. Title pages will be prepared in manuscript.

Place	Date	Hour	Summary of Events and Information	Remarks and references to Appendices
VOX VRIE	Sept 1		PTE WRIGHT reports from leave. Admitted 24 animals, & evacuated 21 to XIV Corps S&S	
"	2		1 animal discharged, cured, to 142 Hy Batty. 29 animals admitted, & 25 evacuated to Corps S&S	
"	3		Admitted 15 animals, & evacuated 26 to Corps S&S	
"	4		Sent two strays horses to 2/3/B DAC. Admitted 8 animals, & evacuated 14 to Corps S&S	
"			Pte Hadin proud on leave to Scotland	
"	5		Admitted 15 animals, & evacuated 2 to Corps S&S	
"	6		1 animal discharged cured to A Batt 122 R F A. Admitted 12 animals & evacuated 21 to Corps S&S	
"	7		14 animals received, & 11 evacuated to Corps S&S	
"	8		18 animals received, & 16 evacuated to Corps S&S	
"	9		24 animals received, 1 died, & 17 evacuated to Corps S&S	
"	10		10 animals received, & 23 evacuated to Corps S&S. Advanced party signed Sister	
"	11		4 animals received. Left VOX VRIE at 9.45 am arrived PROVEN 11-30 am	
PROVEN	12		13 animals received, & 11 evacuated to Corps S&S 2 horses to 18th MVS	
"	13		Evacuated 14 animals to Corps S&S. Left PROVEN 10-30 am, arrived EECKE 5-0 pm	
EECKE	14		Left EECKE 9-0 am arriving STEINBECK 3-0 pm	
STEINBECK	15		Left STEINBECK 9-45 am. Arrive G14 C 2-4 at 4-0 pm & take up billet with 2/1 Lanes MVS	

Army Form C. 2118.

WAR DIARY
or
INTELLIGENCE SUMMARY.
(Erase heading not required.)

Instructions regarding War Diaries and Intelligence Summaries are contained in F. S. Regs., Part II. and the Staff Manual respectively. Title pages will be prepared in manuscript.

Place	Date	Hour	Summary of Events and Information	Remarks and references to Appendices
EPINETTE	SEPT 16		Hour Shot proceed to EECKE to relieve horse of Divisional Artillery	
"	17		2 animals sold to Butcher. Shot returns from EECKE	
"	18		8 animals evacuated by Barge to 23 D/VH. PTE CARR proceed on leave PTE HARDIE	returns from leave
"	19		6 animals admitted	
"	20		8 animals admitted, + 1 horse returned to M M T for Duty	
"	21		2 animals admitted + 12 evacuated by Barge to 23 D/VH	
"	22		Inspection of Rifles + Gas Helmets	
"	23		5 animals admitted	
"	24		13 animals admitted	
"	25		24 animals evacuated by Barge to 23 D/VH	
"	26		5 animals admitted	
"	27		3 animals admitted, + 1 sold to Butcher	
"	28		3 animals admitted, + 7 evacuated by Barge to 23 D/VH	
"	29		2 animals admitted. Inspection of rifles + gas helmets	
"	30		4 animals admitted. Pte BOWEN proceed on leave to England. Pte CARR returns from leave	

1-16-17

Paul Johns Capt AVC
4th MVS

Vol 23

CONFIDENTIAL WAR DIARY

OF

CAPT. P. HOWARD AVC

No 49 MOBILE VETERINARY SECTION

VOL XXIII

FROM OCT. 1ST TO OCT 31ST

Army Form C. 2118.

WAR DIARY
or
INTELLIGENCE SUMMARY.
(Erase heading not required.)

Instructions regarding War Diaries and Intelligence Summaries are contained in F.S. Regs., Part II. and the Staff Manual respectively. Title pages will be prepared in manuscript.

Place	Date	Hour	Summary of Events and Information	Remarks and references to Appendices
SHEET 36 G14 C 2-4	Oct			
	1		11 animals admitted – 2 sold for slaughter	
	2		1 animal admitted, 1 sold for slaughter & 18 evacuated to Vet Hospital	
	3		1 animal admitted & 1 sold for slaughter	
	4		5 animals admitted	
	5		1 mule collected from inhabitant at DOULIEU & 5 been evacuated	
	6		3 animals admitted & 2 sold for slaughter. Inspection of Rifles & Gas Helmets	
	7		1 animal admitted	
	8		4 animals admitted	
	9		8 animals evacuated to Vet Hospital & 1 sold for slaughter	
	10		3 animals admitted	
	11		5 animals admitted	
	12		2 animals admitted, & 8 evacuated to Vet Hospital. PTE BOWEN reports from leave	
	13		2 animals admitted. Inspection of Rifles & Gas Helmets. PTE HILL proceeds on leave	
	14		2 animals admitted, & 4 horses for treatment suffering from OPHTH & MIT	
	15		3 animals admitted	
	16		1 animal admitted & 11 evacuated to Vet Hospital. 1 mule to Field Remount Station	

Army Form C. 2118.

WAR DIARY
or
INTELLIGENCE SUMMARY.
(Erase heading not required.)

Instructions regarding War Diaries and Intelligence Summaries are contained in F. S. Regs., Part II. and the Staff Manual respectively. Title pages will be prepared in manuscript.

Place	Date	Hour	Summary of Events and Information	Remarks and references to Appendices
SHEET 36 C 4 C 2-4	Oct			
	17		3 animals admitted & 1 destroyed. Capt Howard proceeds on leave	
	18		4 animals admitted	
	19		1 animal admitted	
	20		5 animals admitted Inspection of Rifles & gas Helmets	
	21		2 horses sent for shoeing	
	22		1 animal admitted	
	23		1 animal admitted & 11 evacuated to 23rd Vet Hospital	
	24		2 animals admitted & 1 destroyed	
	25		6 animals admitted. PTE HILL reports from leave	
	26		3 animals admitted & 1 destroyed	
	27		2 animals admitted PTE WOODS proceeds on leave. Inspection of Rifles & gas Helmets	
	28		12 animals admitted	
	29		11 animals admitted Captain Howard returns from leave	
	30		7 animals admitted & 27 evacuated to 23rd Vet Hospital	
	31		14 animals admitted & 1 destroyed for duty	Pack Mules Lyr A/C M. 49th MTS 31-b-17

Vol 24

Confidential War Diary

of

Capt P Howard AVC

No 49 Mobile Veterinary Section

Vol XXIV

From Nov 1st 1917 To Nov 30th 1917

WAR DIARY
or
INTELLIGENCE SUMMARY.
(Erase heading not required.)

Army Form C. 2118.

Place	Date	Hour	Summary of Events and Information	Remarks and references to Appendices
SHEET 36	Nov			
C14c2-4	1		Admitted 15 animals & turned 2 to 169th Bgde	
"	2		Admitted 4 animals & returned 2 to 38th DAC. Evacuated 35 animals to 23rd Veterinary Hospital. S/Sgt HUGHES proceeds on leave to UK	
"	3		Inspection of Rifles & Gas Helmets	
"	4		Inspection of Gastring	
"	5		Admitted 14 animals & divising 2 to D 122 Bde for duty	
"	6		Admitted 2 animals. S/Sgt ANDERSON & 12 men proceed to MERVILLE for Horse Sale	
"	7		Admitted 13 animals & evacuated 19 to 23rd V.H. Horse Sale party returned	
"	8		Admitted 12 animals. PTE WOODS reports from Leave	
"	9		Admitted 5 animals & evacuated 25 to 23rd V.H. 5 ORs dispatched to LE HAVRE for transfer	
"	10		Admitted 4 animals. Inspection of Rifles & Gas Helmets	
"	11		Admitted 3 animals. Inspection of Buty mana	
"	12		Admitted 7 animals & divising 1 to HQRS for duty	
"	13		Admitted 1 animals & evacuated 18 to 23rd V.H. 1 Horse to Butcher	
"	14		Admitted 7 animals	

Army Form C. 2118

WAR DIARY
or
INTELLIGENCE SUMMARY
(Erase heading not required.)

Instructions regarding War Diaries and Intelligence Summaries are contained in F. S. Regs., Part II. and the Staff Manual respectively. Title Pages will be prepared in manuscript.

Place	Date	Hour	Summary of Events and Information	Remarks and references to Appendices
SHEET 36 G.W.C.2-4	Nov 15		Admitted 7 animals	
	16		Admitted 6 animals & evacuated 15 to 23rd V.H.	
	17		Admitted 2 animals. Inspection of Rifles & Gas helmets	
	18		S/Sgt HUGHES return from leave	
	19		Admitted 10 animals. PTE DUCKWORTH proceeds on leave to UK	
	20		Admitted 2 animals & evacuated 17 to 23rd V.H.	
	21		Admitted 5 animals	
	22		Admitted 5 animals. 2 ord to Butchers	
	23		Admitted 1 animal. evacuated 6 to 23rd V.H.	
	24		Admitted 8 animals	
	25		Lindsay on loan for duty to 332 Co ASC	
	26		Admitted 4 animals	
	27		Admitted 4 animals. S/Sgt ANDERSON proceeds on leave to UK	
	28		Admitted 3 animals. 1 collected from NEUF. BERQUIN, to 1 from	
	29		Admitted 5 animals (VIEUX BERQUIN)	
			1 collected from MERRIS	
	30		Admitted animals. evacuated 13 to 23rd V.H.	

Rev. Hawes Capt. A.V.C.
O.C. 49th MVS

WD 25

Confidential War Diary
of

Capt P Howard AVC

No 49 Mobile Veterinary Section

Vol XXV

From Dec 1st To Dec 31st

Army Form C. 2118.

WAR DIARY
or
INTELLIGENCE SUMMARY.
(Erase heading not required.)

Place	Date	Hour	Summary of Events and Information	Remarks and references to Appendices
SHEET 36 C1 4 C.2-4	DEC 1		Admitted 8 animals. Inspection of Rifles & Gas Helmets	
"	2		Admitted 6 animals	
"	3		Admitted 40 animals. PTE MARRIOTT proceeds on leave to UK	
"	4		Admitted 30 animals & evacuated 34 to 23 M/H	
"	5		Admitted 13 animals	
"	6		Admitted 6 animals. PTE SUTTON proceeds on leave	
"	7		Admitted 10 animals. PTE MASON proceeds on leave. 35 animals evacuated	
"	8		Admitted 10 animals. Inspection of Rifles & Gas Helmets	
"	9		Admitted 3 animals	
"	10		Admitted 13 animals	
"	11		Admitted 3 & evacuated 65 animals to 23 M/H. Inspection of Gas Helmets by DDVR	
"	12		Admitted 11 animals. CPL PANTER proceeds on leave to UK	
"	13		Admitted 10 animals. S.SGT SANDERSON reports from leave	
"	14		Admitted 8 & evacuated 13 animals to 23 M/H. PTE ACRES proceeds to UK	
"	15		Admitted 13 animals. Inspection of Rifles & Gas Helmets	

49th MOBILE VETERINARY SECTION.
No. ....
Date 1-1-18

Army Form C. 2118.

WAR DIARY
or
INTELLIGENCE SUMMARY.
(Erase heading not required.)

Instructions regarding War Diaries and Intelligence Summaries are contained in F.S. Regs., Part II. and the Staff Manual respectively. Title pages will be prepared in manuscript.

Place **SHEET 36** G.H.Q-C.R-4 16

Date Dec	Hour	Summary of Events and Information	Remarks and references to Appendices
16		Admitted 4 animals	
17		Admitted 5 animals	
18		Admitted 11 animals & evacuated 22 to No 23 V/H. 4 animals returned to unit for duty PTE CLARKE proceeds on leave to U.K. Sgt SMITH proceeds to ROUEN for duty	
19		Admitted 8 & destroyed 1	
20		Admitted 16 animals & discharged 1 to duty	
21		Admitted 2 animals	
22		Evacuated 27 animals to 23 V/H, & discharged 2 for duty PTE SUTTON reports for duty	
23		Admitted 7 animals PTE PITS.N, & PTE ROBINSON proceed on leave to UK	
		PTE MASON reports for duty	
24		Admitted 4 animals, & discharged 2 for duty	
25		Admitted 1 animal	
26		Admitted 6 animals & discharged 2 for duty	
27		Admitted 11 animals	
28		Admitted 5 animals & evacuated 33 to 23 V/H. Sgt PANTER reports from leave	
29		Admitted 10 animals to discharged 1 for duty. Inspector of Rifles & gas helmets	
30		Admitted 2 animals PTE ACRES reports from leave	
31		Admitted 4 animals & discharged 2 for duty	

Pun/Stewart Capt. A.V.C.
O.C. 49th MVS.

1-1-18

M 26

CONFIDENTIAL WAR DIARY

OF

CAPTAIN P HOWARD AVC.

No 49 MOBILE VETERINARY SECTION

VOL XXVI

FROM JANUARY 1 TO JANUARY 31
1918

Army Form C. 2118.

WAR DIARY
or
INTELLIGENCE SUMMARY
(Erase heading not required.)

Instructions regarding War Diaries and Intelligence Summaries are contained in F. S. Regs., Part II. and the Staff Manual respectively. Title pages will be prepared in manuscript.

Place	Date	Hour	Summary of Events and Information	Remarks and references to Appendices
SHEET 36 C.14.C.4.4	Jan 1		4 animals admitted, 1 discharged to duty	
" "	2		7 animals admitted, 2 discharged to duty	
" "	3		19 animals admitted	
" "	4		4 animals admitted, 36 evacuated to 23rd V.H.	
" "	5		4 animals admitted, 3 discharged to duty. PTE CLARKE reports from leave Inspection of Rifles & gas helmets	
" "	6		1 animal admitted. CPL SAYLOR proceeds on leave to UK	
" "	7		18 animals admitted, 3 discharged to duty	
" "	8		10 animals admitted, 31 evacuated to 23rd V.H. PTE ROLLINSON reports from leave	
" "	9		12 animals admitted, 8 discharged to duty	
" "	10		11 animals admitted. PTE PITSON reports from leave	
" "	11		4 animals admitted, 2 discharged to duty	
" "	12		10 animals admitted, 33 evacuated to 23 V.H.	
" "	13		5 animals admitted, 3 discharged to duty. Inspection of Rifles & Gun helmets	
" "	14		15 animals admitted	
" "	15		1 animal admitted. 29 evacuated to 23rd V.H. Moved off from L'EPINETTE at 1-30 p.m. 11-30 a.m. arrived MERVILLE - (RECMER-LECLERCQ)	

Army Form C. 2118.

WAR DIARY
or
INTELLIGENCE SUMMARY
(Erase heading not required.)

Instructions regarding War Diaries and Intelligence Summaries are contained in F. S. Regs., Part II. and the Staff Manual respectively. Title pages will be prepared in manuscript.

Place	Date	Hour	Summary of Events and Information	Remarks and references to Appendices
RECQUIER	16		1 animal discharged to duty	
LECLERCQ	17		1 animal admitted. Inspection of Rifles & Saddlery	
"	18		1 animal admitted	
"	19		16 animals admitted	
"	20		Inspection of Rifles & Gas Helmets	
"	21		24 animals admitted, 1 a strays	
"	22		2 animals admitted. 42 animals evacuated to 13 V.H	
"	23		1 animal admitted. Cpl YALLOP upto from leave	
"	24		1 animal admitted	
"	25		2 animals admitted	
"	26		6 animals admitted, 2 discharged to duty. Inspection of Rifles & Gas Helmets	
"	27		16 animals admitted	
"	28		13 animals admitted	
"	29		10 animals admitted. 29 evacuated to 13 V.H	
"	30		7 animals admitted, 3 mules issued, 1 destroyed	
"	31		5 animals admitted. Horse Ambulance taken to Ordnance workshop (broken down)	

P Hues Capt A.V.C
O.C. 49th M.V.S

49th MOBILE
VETERINARY
SECTION
Date 1.2.18

14 49 Mob Vty Sec
    38 Division

Vol 27

CONFIDENTIAL.

WAR DIARY

OF

CAPT P. HOWARD AVC

No 49 MOBILE VETERINARY SECTION

Vol XXVII

FROM FEB 1ST TO FEB 28TH 1918

Army Form C. 2118.

WAR DIARY
or
INTELLIGENCE SUMMARY.
(Erase heading not required.)

Instructions regarding War Diaries and Intelligence Summaries are contained in F.S. Regs., Part II. and the Staff Manual respectively. Title pages will be prepared in manuscript.

Place	Date	Hour	Summary of Events and Information	Remarks and references to Appendices
REGNIER-LECLERCQ (NORD)	FEB 1		1 animal admitted, 23 evacuated to 13 Vet Hospital by rail	
"	2		11 animals admitted, 1 issued to 114 Bde H Q Rs. Inspection of Rifles & Gas Helmets	
"	3		1 animal discharged for duty (16th Welsh)	
"	4		22 animals admitted, 2 discharged to duty, (2S DAC) Cpl. Bond proceeded to UK on leave	
"	5		9 animals admitted	
"	6		1 animal admitted, 1 discharged to duty (A121) 27 evacuated to 13 Vet Hospital by rail	
"	7		4 animals admitted	
"	9		2 animals admitted Inspection of Rifles & Gas Helmets	
"	10		3 animals admitted	
"	11		4 animals admitted	
"	12		10 animals admitted	
"	13		4 animals admitted	
"	14		4 animals admitted, 39 evacuated to 13 Vet Hospital by rail	
"	16		Moved off at 10.45 am. ARRIVED STEENWERCK at 3.0 pm. Left 3 animals with 2/1 LANCS MVS. in old billet & took over 14 animals from same in new billet.	

Army Form C. 2118.

WAR DIARY
or
INTELLIGENCE SUMMARY.
(Erase heading not required.)

Instructions regarding War Diaries and Intelligence Summaries are contained in F.S. Regs., Part II. and the Staff Manual respectively. Title pages will be prepared in manuscript.

Place	Date FEB	Hour	Summary of Events and Information	Remarks and references to Appendices
STEENWERCK	18		18 animals smitted	
"	19		9 animals smitted, 11 evacuated to 23rd Vet Hospital by tray.	
"	20		8 animals smitted	
"	21		7 animals smitted. Cpl BONB expert from here to UK	
"	22		4 animals smitted, 30 evacuated to 23rd Vet Hospital by tray.	
"	23		5 animals smitted	
"	24		7 animals smitted	
"	25		11 animals smitted. 1 dinkey to 130th Field Ambulance for duty. Inspection of Rifles & Gas Helmets	
"	26		4 animals smitted, 20 evacuated to 13th Vet Hospital by tray.	
"	27		2 animals smitted	
"	28		4 animals smitted 2 - 3 - 18	

Geo Anderson Capt AVC
F.49 M.V.S

Vol 28

Confidential War Diary

of

Captain A. Young, AVC.

No 49 Mobile Veterinary Section
38 Division

Vol XXVIII

From March 1st To March 31st

Army Form C. 2118.

WAR DIARY
or
INTELLIGENCE SUMMARY.
(Erase heading not required.)

Instructions regarding War Diaries and Intelligence Summaries are contained in F. S. Regs., Part II. and the Staff Manual respectively. Title pages will be prepared in manuscript.

Place	Date	Hour	Summary of Events and Information	Remarks and references to Appendices
	March			
STEENWERCK	1		2 animals admitted, 25 evacuated to 23 Vet Hospital (By Barge)	
"	2		Capt. A. Young AVC arrived & took over command of Section vice Capt P. HOWARD	
"			transferred to XV Corps V.E.S. 8 animals admitted. Nos 30 & 812 PTE YOUNG found Section	
"	3		4 animals admitted	
"	4		6 animals admitted, 1 discharged to duty	
"	5		3 animals admitted, 11 evacuated to 23 Vet Hospital (By Barge)	
"	6		11 animals admitted	
"	7		4 animals admitted	
"	8		11 animals evacuated to 23 Vet Hospital (By Barge)	
"	9		5 animals admitted, 3 discharged to duty. Inspection of Rifles & Gas Helmets	
"	10		4 animals admitted, PTE HOLT proceed on leave to UK	
"	11		8 animals admitted, 1 discharged to duty	
"	12		8 animals admitted, 10 evacuated to 23 Vet Hospital (By Barge)	
"	13		5 animals admitted	
"	14		20 animals admitted	
"	15		2 animals admitted, 30 evacuated to 23 Vet Hospital, 2 discharged to duty	
			PTE CRANDON proceed on leave to UK	A.Y.

Army Form C. 2118.

WAR DIARY
or
INTELLIGENCE SUMMARY.
(Erase heading not required.)

Instructions regarding War Diaries and Intelligence Summaries are contained in F.S. Regs., Part II. and the Staff Manual respectively. Title pages will be prepared in manuscript.

Place	Date	Hour	Summary of Events and Information	Remarks and references to Appendices
STEENWERCK	March 16		5 animals Destroyed - Inspection of Rifles + Gas Helmets	
"	17		7 animals Destroyed, 2 Discharged to duty	
"	18		5 animals Destroyed, 2 Discharged to duty	
"	19		1 animal Destroyed	
"	20		3 animals Destroyed. No.SE.11540 Pte MASON AVC transferred to No 1 CONVALESCENT HORSE DEPOT for duty.	
"	21		7 animals Destroyed, 7 Discharged to duty	
"	22		3 animals Destroyed, 6 evacuated to 23 MVS, 2 Discharged to duty. DVR EDWARDS proceeded on leave to UK	
"	23		10 animals Destroyed. Inspection of Rifles T.C. as Helmets	
"	24		5 animals Destroyed. DR EDWARDS expires Section. (Leave cancelled)	
"	25		3 animals Destroyed.	
"	26		5 animals Destroyed. PTE HOLT reports from leave.	
"	27		3 animals Destroyed, 21 evacuated to XV Corps V.E.S. (By Rly)	
"	28		2 animals Discharged to duty	
"	29		3 animals Destroyed, 11 evacuated to XV C.V.E.S., 12 discharged to duty.	
"	30		4 animals Destroyed, 6 L.O.D. rec'd to 24 MVS. Moved off from STEENWERCK 11.0 PM ARRIVED MERVILLE 3.0 PM	
MERVILLE	31		Nil	

A. Young Capt. AVC.

40th MOBILE VETERINARY SECTION.
1-4-18

A5834 Wt. W4973 M687 750,000 8/16 D.D.&L.Ltd. Forms/C.2118/13.

17.

Vol 29

CONFIDENTIAL WAR DIARY

OF

CAPTAIN A. YOUNG. A.V.C.

No. 49 MOBILE VETY. SECTION

VOL. XXIX.

FROM APRIL 1st 1918 TO APRIL 30th 1918

Army Form C. 2118.

WAR DIARY
or
INTELLIGENCE SUMMARY.
(Erase heading not required.)

Place	Date	Hour	Summary of Events and Information	Remarks and references to Appendices
MERVILLE	1-4-18		Left MERVILLE, 4.15 P.M. Arrived STEENBECQUE 8 p.m., entrained for 11.0 p.m. left	
	2.4.18		STEENBECQUE 11.30 p.m.	
DOULLENS			Arrived DOULLENS 7.0 a.m. Left DOULLENS 9.0 a.m. arrived TOUTENCOURT 3.30 p.m.	
	3-4-18		1 animal admitted (Bde GEN PHILLIPS Charger.)	
	4.4.18		2 animals admitted.	
	5.4.18		5 animals admitted.	
	5.4.18		15 Animals admitted, 7 Animals evacuated to II Corps Veterinary Evacuating Station (Sgt MUNNULLY in charge.)	
	6.4.18		7 Animals admitted, Section proc. to H.Q., one returned to 331.10.A.S.C., 1 Destroyed.	
	7.4.18		One animal died, seven animals evacuated, SGT MUNNULLY in charge.	
	8.4.18		5 animals admitted, Rifle inspection	
	9.4.18		5 animals admitted	
	10.4.18		2 animals admitted	

WAR DIARY or INTELLIGENCE SUMMARY.

Army Form C. 2118.

(Erase heading not required.)

Place	Date	Hour	Summary of Events and Information	Remarks and references to Appendices
DOULLENS	11-4-18		(Cont) 14 animals admitted, one animal issued to 333 Co. A.S.C.	
"	12-4-18		1 animal admitted, 8 animals evacuated to I Corps Veterinary Evacuation Station	
"	13-4-18		4 animals admitted, 1 stray issued to 10th S.W.B., 8 animals evacuated. Inspection of Rifles	
"	14-4-18		6 animals admitted, 1 stray admitted (Enemy)	
"	15-4-18		4 animals admitted, 8 animals evacuated.	
"	16-4-18		3 animals admitted, 1 Issuer to 333 Co. A.S.C., 1 Destroyed (TETANUS) 1 Returned to 17th Bn. R.W.F.	
"	17-4-18		1 animal admitted, 1 Horse Died (123 Field Co. R.E.)	
"	18-4-18		5 animals admitted, 1 Returned to 114th Inf. Bde.	
"	19-4-18		15 animals admitted, 6 evacuated, 1 stray horse sent to A.P.M. 38th Div.	
"	20-4-18		13 animals admitted, 14 animals Evacuated, 2 animals destroyed, 1 animal Returned to H.Q. 115th (Coy)	
"	21-4-18		4 animals admitted, 11 animals evacuated.	
"	22-4-18		2 animals admitted	
"	23-4-18		10 animals admitted.	
"	24-4-18		9 animals admitted, 10 animals evacuated to I Corps V.E.S. SGT. PANTER 1/c., 1 animal died belonging to 122 Hy. Bty. R.G.A.	
"	25-4-18		2 animals destroyed, 8 animals evacuated.	
"	26-4-18		2 animals admitted, 14 animals evacuated.	
"	27-4-18		11 animals admitted, one animal destroyed. Inspection of Hot Respirators & Rifles, ek.	

Army Form C. 2118.

WAR DIARY
or
INTELLIGENCE SUMMARY.
(Erase heading not required.)

Instructions regarding War Diaries and Intelligence Summaries are contained in F.S. Regs., Part II. and the Staff Manual respectively. Title pages will be prepared in manuscript.

Place	Date	Hour	Summary of Events and Information	Remarks and references to Appendices
DOULLENS	28.4.18		8 animals admitted, 11 animals evacuated, 8 Sgt. ANDERSON in charge	
"	29.4.18		15 animals admitted; One returned to 130th Field Ambulance, Two animals evacuated by horse ambulance	
"	30.4.18		One animal admitted. Two stray animals returned to 123rd Field Co R.E.	

A. Young
Capt. A.V.C.
O.C. No. 49 Mobile Veterinary Section

49th MOBILE
VETERINARY
SECTION.
No. ....
Date ....

No 30

17

Original

Confidential War Diary

of

Capt. A. Young. A.V.C.

O.C. 49 Mobile Veterinary Section

Volume XXX

From May 1st 1918   To May 31st 1918

Army Form C. 2118.

WAR DIARY
or
INTELLIGENCE SUMMARY.
(Erase heading not required.)

Instructions regarding War Diaries and Intelligence Summaries are contained in F. S. Regs., Part II. and the Staff Manual respectively. Title pages will be prepared in manuscript.

Place	Date	Hour	Summary of Events and Information	Remarks and references to Appendices
TOUTENCOURT	May 1st 1918		One animal admitted	
"	2-19.18		Two animals admitted. Two animals Evacuated to No 5. V.E.S., One Horse sent to A.P.M. 38th Division. PTE. PITSON A.V.C. proceeds to No 2 Valy. Hospital.	
"	3-5-18		Two animals admitted. One mule sent to C. Coy. 38th Bn M.G.C.	
"	4-5-18		Seven animals admitted. Two horses returned to 151 Field A. R.E. One section horse sent to 38th D.H.Q. Inspection of Rifles and Box Respirators.	
"	5-5-18		4 Animals admitted. 13 Animals Evacuated to No 5. V.E.S.	
"	6-5-18		2 Animals admitted.	
"	7-5-18		5 Animals admitted.	
"	8-5-18		6 animals admitted. 2 Animals Evacuated to No 5. V.E.S. One horse returned to 131st = FIELD AMBULANCE. Inspection of Box Respirators.	
"	9-5-18		5 animals admitted. 14 Animals Evacuated to No 5 V.E.S. PTE. ACRE'S Taken came down; PTE ACRES admitted to Hospital.	
"	10-5-18		One animal admitted.	A.F.
"	11-5-18		Inspection of Rifles, Steel helmets, & Box Respirators.	

A5834 Wt. W4973/M687 750,000 8/16 D. D. & L. Ltd. Forms/C.2118/13.

Army Form C. 2118.

WAR DIARY
or
INTELLIGENCE SUMMARY.
(Erase heading not required.)

Instructions regarding War Diaries and Intelligence Summaries are contained in F. S. Regs., Part II. and the Staff Manual respectively. Title pages will be prepared in manuscript.

Place	Date	Hour	Summary of Events and Information	Remarks and references to Appendices
TOUTENCOURT	12-5-18		Sit	
"	13-5-18		10 Animals admitted, one animal destroyed, of 124 Field Co R.E.	
"	14-5-18		4 Animals admitted, 14 Animals Evacuated to No. 5 V.E.S. (SGT PANTER i/c) PTE CLARKE, PTE MARSHALL, PTE SUTTON, PTE WOODS, proceed to No. 2 Veterinary Hospital. S.SGT ANDERSON proceeds on reengagement leave.	
"	15-5-18		One Animal admitted.	
"	16-5-18		Sit	
"	17-5-18		3 Animals Evacuated to No. 5 V.E.S. (PTE BREWSTER i/c) 2 Animals admitted	
"	18-5-18		One horse admitted to 14th Bn. R.W.F., 7 Animals admitted, Inspection of Ruffles't Post Refrigeration	
"	19-5-18		7 Animals admitted. PTE LITTLE, PTE HOLT, and Capt Young forward to PARIS to undergo instruction. Lieutenant W. Preston instring.	
"	20-5-18		2 Sick horses Evacuated (by sick horse ambulance) to No. 5 V.E.S.	
"	21-5-18		11 Animals admitted.	
"	22-5-18		3 animals admitted, CAPTAIN COOMBS, F.M. A.V.C. takes charge of 49th M.V.S.	
"	23-5-18		Evacuated 12 Animals to No. 4 V.E.S. CPL. YALLOR i/c	A.Y.

Army Form C. 2118.

WAR DIARY
or
INTELLIGENCE SUMMARY.

(Erase heading not required.)

Instructions regarding War Diaries and Intelligence Summaries are contained in F.S. Regs., Part II. and the Staff Manual respectively. Title pages will be prepared in manuscript.

Place	Date	Hour	Summary of Events and Information	Remarks and references to Appendices
TOUTENCOURT	24-5-18		3 Animals admitted. One horse issued to 15th Bn Welsh Regt., one horse issued to 123 Field Co. R.E., One horse issued to 14th Bn. R.W.F.	
"	25-5-18		7 Animals admitted, 7 Animals evacuated to No. 4. V.E.S. Cpl. Bond. V/c., One horse evacuated (vy float) to No. 4. V.E.S. Inspection of Rifles and Box Respirators.	
	26-5-18		2 Animals admitted	
	27-5-18		10 Animals admitted., Pte Little and Pte. Holt and Pte. Young. return from Paris. Captain Young. A.V.C. takes charge of 49th M.V.S., Captain Coombs proceeds to Doullens.	
	28-5-18		One horse evacuated (vy float) to No. 4. V.E.S., One horse destroyed of 2/1 Lancs. Bty. R.G.A.	
	29-5-18		6 Animals admitted.	
	30-5-18		2 Animals admitted for treatment, 5 horses evacuated to No. 4. V.E.S.	
	31-5-18		15 Animals admitted	

A. Young. Capt. A.V.C.
O.C. No. 49 Mobile Vety. Section

14

Vol 31

Original

Confidential War Diary

of

Captain A. Young. A.V.C.

49th Mobile Veterinary Section

From June 1st 1918 — To June 30th 1918

Army Form C. 2118.

WAR DIARY
or
INTELLIGENCE SUMMARY.
(Erase heading not required.)

Instructions regarding War Diaries and Intelligence Summaries are contained in F. S. Regs., Part II. and the Staff Manual respectively. Title pages will be prepared in manuscript.

Place	Date	Hour	Summary of Events and Information	Remarks and references to Appendices
TOUTENCOURT	1/6/18		Seven animals admitted. Inspection of Boot Reparators, Rifles, Steel Helmets, & Spurs at 9a.m.	15 Animals Evacuated to No 5 V.E.S.
"	2/6/18		Twelve animals admitted.	
"	3/6/18		Five animals admitted. Twelve animals evacuated to No. 5. V.E.S. CPL. YALLOP ½.	
"	4/6/18		Five animals admitted.	
"	5/6/18		Twelve animals evacuated to No. 5. V.E.S. SGT. PANTER ½., 3 animals admitted.	
"	6/6/18		Two animals admitted, Turn of 49th M.V.S. paid at 6.0 p.m.	
"	7/6/18		Three animals admitted and Two stray animals received from A.P.M. 38th Division.	
"	8/6/18		Six animals admitted. Two stray animals claimed by D/315 Bn A.T.A. Inspection of Boot Reparators, Rifles, & Steel Helmets, One stray mule Received from 2nd Garrison Batt. K.O.Y.L.I.	
"	9/6/18		One horse of 130th Field Ambulance discharged fit for duty. Two animals admitted.	
"	10/6/18		Ten animals evacuated to No. 5. V.E.S. CPL. BOND ½.	
"	11/6/18		Three animals admitted.	
"	12/6/18		Ten animals admitted.	
"	13/6/18		Ten animals admitted. Twenty two animals evacuated to No. 5. V.E.S. SGT. PANTER ½.	

WAR DIARY or INTELLIGENCE SUMMARY

Army Form C. 2118.

Place	Date	Hour	Summary of Events and Information	Remarks and references to Appendices
TINTENCOURT	14/6/18		Received one stray animal from 38th Divisional Signal Co., one animal admitted sick.	
"	15/6/18		Inspection of Rifles, Box Respirators, and Steel helmets at 9 a.m. Two animals evacuated to No. 4 V.E.S. by Sick horse Ambulance.	
"	16/6/18		Seven animals admitted, Ten animals evacuated to No. 5. V.E.S. CPL. BOND. /c.	
"	17/6/18		Four men temporarily withdrawn from 49th M.V.S. animal strength, one Rider issued to 15th (Batt. Welsh Regt.), one Rider issued to 16th Batt. R.W.F., one Rider since to 17th Bn R.W.F.	
"	18/6/18		One Rider issued to H.Q. 113 Infantry Bde.	
"	19/6/18		5 animals admitted.	
"	20/6/18		Inspection of saddlery at 3.30 p.m.	
"			Three animals admitted, Paid sum of 49th M.V.S. at 6.0 p.m., 16 animals evacuated to No. 5 V.E.S.	
"	21/6/18		One Stray animal admitted (Issued to 178 Tunnelling Co. R.E.) STAFF SGT ANDERSON returned from re-engagement leave. Four animals admitted.	
"	22/6/18		Four animals admitted, Inspection of Rifles, Steel helmets, Box Respirators & Wallets. (Veterinary) S. SGT. ANDERSON. Proceeded to No. 15 V.E.S. for duty.	
"	23/6/18		Twelve animals evacuated to No. 5. V.E.S. CPL YALLOP /c., 3 animals admitted.	
"	24/6/18		Fourteen animals admitted.	
"	25/6/18		Sixteen animals evacuated to No. 5 V.E.S., S. SMITH. HUGHES. reported sick (Extended duty for 2 days)	

WAR DIARY
or
INTELLIGENCE SUMMARY.

(Erase heading not required.)

Army Form C. 2118.

Place	Date	Hour	Summary of Events and Information	Remarks and references to Appendices
TOUTENCOURT	26/8/18		Three animals admitted sick and one mule (stray) PTE TARREN & PTE WAITE reported sick. (sick excused duty 2 days)	
"	27/8/18		S.S. HUGHES. light duty 2 days., Nine animals admitted, ten animals evacuated to 5. V.E.S.	
"	28/8/18		Sgt PANTER, PTE. BOLT, PTE WASH, & Dr ANTHONY reported sick, (all excused duty 2 days) PTE TARREN & PTE WAITE (light duty) PTE. BITSON reported sick. (excused duty 2 days)	
"	29/8/18		SGT. MUNNULLY, CPL. YALLOP. PTE. NAYLOR reported sick (all excused duty.) Two animals admitted.	
"	30/8/18		4 animals admitted, SGT. PANTER, PTE. WASH, PTE. TARREN, PTE. WAITE, returned to duty.	

A. Young Capt Tower
O.C. 49 M.V.S.

38

11

Vol 32

Confidential War Diary
of
Capt N. Young. M.C.

H.Q. 4th Mobile Veterinary Section

From July 1st 1918   To. July 31st 1918

WAR DIARY
or
INTELLIGENCE SUMMARY
(Erase heading not required.)

Army Form C. 2118.

Place	Date	Hour	Summary of Events and Information	Remarks and references to Appendices
TOTTENCOURT	1/7/18		Six animals admitted.	
"	2/7/18		Three animals admitted. Inspection of rifles and Box Respirators at 9.0 am	
"	3/7/18		Three animals admitted, one animal evacuated by float to 9.5 V.E.S.	
"	4/7/18		Admitted 2 animals. Twelve animals evacuated to 9.5 V.E.S. Cpl. YALLOP 1/e	
"	5/7/18		Admitted one animal. Destroyed on arrival of H.Q. 113 Bde.	
"	6/7/18		Thirteen animals admitted. Inspection of rifles & Box Respirators at 9.0 am	
"	7/7/18		Evacuated eight animals to 9.5 V.E.S. Cpl. BOND 1/e	
"	8/7/18		Three animals admitted.	
"	9/7/18		One animal admitted, one animal evacuated by float to 9.5 V.E.S.	
"	10/7/18		Two animals admitted. Box Respirators worn from 2.0 pm to 3 pm.	
"	11/7/18		Six animals admitted. Box Respirators worn from 6.0 am to 7.0 am.	
"	12/7/18		Two animals admitted. Box Respirators worn from 6.0 am to 7.0 Am.	
"	13/7/18		Ten animals admitted. Box Respirators worn from 6.0 am to 7.0 Am. Inspection of Respirators Rifles	
"	14/7/18		Sixteen animals evacuated to 9.5 V.E.S. One animal admitted. Box Respirators worn from 6.0 am to 7.0 am	
"	ditto		PTE. TARREN, T. Awarded 7 days C.C. and Seven extra piquets.	
"	15/7/18		Two animals admitted. Box Respirators worn from 6.0 am to 7.0 am. Two animals destroyed	A.Y.

Army Form C. 2118.

WAR DIARY
or
INTELLIGENCE SUMMARY.
(Erase heading not required.)

Instructions regarding War Diaries and Intelligence Summaries are contained in F. S. Regs., Part II. and the Staff Manual respectively. Title pages will be prepared in manuscript.

Place	Date	Hour	Summary of Events and Information	Remarks and references to Appendices
TOUTENCOURT	16/7/18		Two animals destroyed, PTE SPRY proceeded on 14 days leave to England, Box Respirators worn from 6.0 am to 7.0 am.	
"	do		Five animals admitted	
"	17/7/18		Seven animals admitted	
"	18/7/18		Six animals admitted	
"	19/7/18		Inspection of Rifles, Box Respirators, Steelhelmets. Private PITSON proceeded to IRELAND for thirty days leave. Thirty Eight animals admitted, 2/n Animals evacuated to N°. 5 V.E.S.	
"	20/7/18			
"	do		Twenty Three animals evacuated to N°. 5 V.E.S. One animal admitted	
"	21/7/18		Eight animals admitted, Three animals destroyed	
"	22/7/18		One animal destroyed belonging to 13.A.C. 93 Bde.A.F.A., One animal admitted	
"	23/7/18		Two animals admitted. Inspection of Box Respirators & Rifles.	
"	24/7/18		Four Animals evacuated to N°. 5 V.E.S. Six animals admitted	
"	25/7/18		Two animals admitted	
"	26/7/18		Destroyed one horse of C/121 Bde R.F.A., Two animals admitted	
"	27/7/18		Three animals admitted	
"	28/7/18			

Army Form C. 2118.

WAR DIARY
or
INTELLIGENCE SUMMARY.
(Erase heading not required.)

Instructions regarding War Diaries and Intelligence Summaries are contained in F. S. Regs., Part II. and the Staff Manual respectively. Title pages will be prepared in manuscript.

Place	Date	Hour	Summary of Events and Information	Remarks and references to Appendices
TUITENCOURT	29/7/18		Seventeen animals evacuated (3 of 49th M.V.S. & 14 of 53rd M.V.S.) Three animals admitted.	
"	30/7/18		One animal evacuated by float, three animals admitted.	
"	31/7/18		Four animals admitted, one animal destroyed of 2/2 32 Bde R.F.A.	

A. Young
Capt. AVC.
O.C. 49th Mobile Veterinary Section

49th MOBILE
VETERINARY
SECTION.

No.............
Date............

26 38

WD 33

CONFIDENTIAL WAR DIARY

OF

CAPT J MACFARLANE AVC

49ᵗʰ MOBILE VETERINARY SECTION

VOL XXXIII

FROM   TO
AUG 1ˢᵀ   AUG 31ˢᵀ

Army Form C. 2118.

WAR DIARY
or
INTELLIGENCE SUMMARY.
(Erase heading not required.)

Instructions regarding War Diaries and Intelligence Summaries are contained in F. S. Regs. Part II. and the Staff Manual respectively. Title pages will be prepared in manuscript.

Place	Date	Hour	Summary of Events and Information	Remarks and references to Appendices
TOUTENCOURT (SOMME)	Aug 1st		8 animals admitted, one destroyed	
"	2		2 animals admitted. PTE Spry return from leave	
"	3		15 animals admitted	
"	4		8 animals admitted. 20 evacuated to 6 V.E.S	
"	5		8 animals admitted. 1 evacuated to 6 V.E.S	
"	6		6 animals admitted. 17 evacuated to 5 V.E.S	
"	7		9 animals admitted. 10 evacuated to 5 V.E.S	
"	8		24 animals admitted	
"	9		8 animals admitted, 1 died. PTE Wash proceed on leave to UK	
"	10		1 animal admitted - 22 evacuated to 5 V.E.S	
"	11		8 animals admitted	
"	12		2 animals destroyed. 4 evacuated by Motor Ambulance to 5 V.E.S	
"	13		3 animals admitted	
"	14		5 animals admitted. DR Edwards proceed on leave to UK	
"	15		3 animals admitted. Capt J MacFarlane AVC relieved Capt Young who proceeding to UK for duty.	

Army Form C. 2118.

WAR DIARY
or
INTELLIGENCE SUMMARY.
(Erase heading not required.)

Instructions regarding War Diaries and Intelligence Summaries are contained in F. S. Regs., Part II. and the Staff Manual respectively. Title pages will be prepared in manuscript.

Place	Date	Hour	Summary of Events and Information	Remarks and references to Appendices
TOUTENCOURT	AUG 16		10 animals admitted. 1 destroyed (including 2 Mules from US Army)	
"	17		12 animals admitted	
"	18		Nil	
"	19		3 animals admitted. PTE TARREN proceeded on leave to UK	
"	20		4 animals admitted	
"	21		6 animals admitted	
"	22		4 animals admitted	
"	23		2 animals admitted	
"	24		4 animals admitted. DR ANTONY proceeded on leave to UK	
VARENNES	25		Left TOUTENCOURT at 3.30pm arrived VARENNES 5.30pm. PTE WASH returned from leave	
"	26		Evacuated 3 animals to 5 V.E.S. Left VARENNES 3.30. arrived BOUZINCOURT 6.0pm	
BOUZINCOURT	27		Admitted 4 animals. Evacuated 4 to 5 V.E.S. Left BOUZINCOURT 3.30pm arrived AVELUY 5.0pm	
AVELUY	28		16 animals admitted	
"	29		4 animals admitted. 14 evacuated to 5 V.E.S	
"	30		15 animals admitted	
"	31		7 animals admitted. 17 evacuated to 5 V.E.S	

John McFarlane
Capt a/c
O/C 49 MVS

49th MOBILE VETERINARY SECTION.
No.
Date. 31-8-18

24 Vol 34

CONFIDENTIAL WAR DIARY

OF

CAPT. J. MACFARLANE A.V.C

49th MOBILE VETERINARY SECTION

VOL XXXIV

FROM 1ST SEPT
TO 30TH SEPT 1918

Army Form C. 2118.

WAR DIARY
or
INTELLIGENCE SUMMARY.
(Erase heading not required.)

Instructions regarding War Diaries and Intelligence Summaries are contained in F. S. Regs., Part II. and the Staff Manual respectively. Title pages will be prepared in manuscript.

Place	Date September	Hour	Summary of Events and Information	Remarks and references to Appendices
AVELUY	1st		Admitted 8 Animals. Evacuated 8 Animals.	
"	2nd		Admitted 4 Animals, Evacuated 4. Moved to CONTALMAISON 2 P.M. arrived 3:30 P.M.	
CONTALMAISON	3rd		Admitted 3 Animals	
"	4th		Admitted 18 Animals. Evacuated 11. Moved to BAZENTIN-LE-PETIT 2 P.M. arrived 3:30 P.M.	
BAZENTIN-LE-PETIT	5th		Admitted 8 Animals. Evacuated 16.	
"	6th		Admitted 13 Animals Evacuated 14.	
"	7		Admitted 8 Animals	
"	8		Admitted 14 Animals. Evacuated 14.	
"	9		Admitted 2 Animals. Evacuated 10. Moved to LE TRANSLOY 10 A.M. arrived 1 P.M.	
LE TRANSLOY	10		Admitted 4 Animals.	
"	11		Admitted 4 Animals.	
"	12		Admitted 4 Animals Evacuated 9 Moved to ROCQUIGNY	
ROCQUIGNY	13		Admitted 4 Animals. Pte Little Leave to U.K.	
"	14		Admitted 12 Animals. Moved to VI.A.8.8. Sheet 57C.	
(Sheet 57(8)) VI.A.8.8.	15		Admitted 4 Animals Evacuated 11 animals	

Army Form C. 2118.

WAR DIARY
or
INTELLIGENCE SUMMARY.
(Erase heading not required.)

Instructions regarding War Diaries and Intelligence Summaries are contained in F. S. Regs., Part II. and the Staff Manual respectively. Title pages will be prepared in manuscript.

Place	Date	Hour	Summary of Events and Information	Remarks and references to Appendices
(Sheet 57.C3) V.I.A.8.8	Sept 2nd 1918	16"	Admitted 5 Animals, Evacuated 2 Animals. Pte WAITE reports from leave	
" "	"	17"	Admitted 16 Animals, Evacuated 2 Animals.	
" "	"	18"	Admitted 15 Animals, Evacuated 16 Animals.	
" "	"	19"	Admitted 10 Animals, Evacuated 13 Animals.	
" "	"	20"	Admitted 10 Animals, Evacuated 2 Animals.	
" "	"	21"	Admitted 22 Animals, Evacuated 21 Animals.	
" "	"	22"	Admitted 21 Animals, Evacuated 15 Animals.	
" "	"	23"	Admitted 6 Animals, Evacuated 13. Sgt MUNNULLY Leave to U.K.	
" "	"	24"	Admitted 11 Animals, Evacuated 6 animals.	
" "	"	25"	Admitted 14 Animals, Evacuated 23 animals.	
" "	"	26"	Admitted 2 Animals, Evacuated 2 Animals.	
" "	"	27"	Admitted 2 Animals, Evacuated 4 Animals.	
" "	"	28"	Admitted 3 Animals, Evacuated 4 Animals. Pte YOUNG proceeds on leave to U.K.	
" "	"	29"	Admitted 6 Animals, Evacuated 8 Animals. (3 cases of Poisoning reduced in Poisoning admittance)	
" "	"	30"	Admitted 3 Animals, Evacuated 1) 3 Gas Poisoning Cases inspected by A.D.V.S. V.Corp	

49th MOBILE VETERINARY SECTION.

John MacFarlane
Capt A.V.C.

30/9/18

Vol 36

CONFIDENTIAL WAR DIARY

OF

Capt. J Macfarlane A.V.C

49th MOBILE VETERINARY SECTION

Volume XXXV

FROM 1st OCTOBER TO 31st OCTOBER

CONFIDENTIAL

WAR DIARY
or
INTELLIGENCE SUMMARY.
(Erase heading not required.)

Army Form C. 2118.

Place	Date October	Hour	Summary of Events and Information	Remarks and references to Appendices
(Sheet 51C) VIASS	1st		Admitted 2 Animals. Evacuated 7 animals. Capt Macfarlane proceeds on leave to U.K.	
FINS	2nd		Moved to FINS 9am to 10.30 am 4 Animals admitted. Capt Pillars takes command of Section	
"	3rd		Admitted 5 Animals. Evacuated 3 animals	
"	4th		Admitted 14 animals. Evacuated 13 Animals	
"	5th		Admitted 9 animals. Evacuated 10 animals	
"	6th		Admitted 4 animals. Pte Naylor proceeds on leave to U.K.	
"	7th		Admitted 7 animals. Evacuated 11 animals	
OsSUs	8th		Moved to OsSUs 9.30am to 12.30 am. 2 animals Admitted 1 Evacuated	
"	9th		Inspection of Rifles & Box Respirators Admitted 5 Evacuated 1 Animals	
MALINCOURT	10th		Moved to MALINCOURT 9.30am to 12.30 am.	
"	11th		Admitted 9 animals. Evacuated 11 Animals	
BERTRY	12th		Moved to BERTRY 9.30 to 1PM. Serg MUNNELLY reported back from U.K.	
"	13th		Admitted 6 animals Evacuated 3 animals	
"	14th		Admitted 3 animals E.	
"	15th		Admitted 9 animals. Evacuated 22 animals	
"	16th		Admitted 7 animals. Evacuated 2 animals	

WAR DIARY
or
INTELLIGENCE SUMMARY.
(Erase heading not required.)

Army Form C. 2118.

Place	Date	Hour	Summary of Events and Information	Remarks and references to Appendices
	October		Continued	
BERTRY	17th		Admitted 19 Animals. Evacuated 32 Animals.	
"	18th		Admitted 29 Animals. Evacuated 9 Animals.	
"	19th		Admitted 15 Animals. Evacuated 25 Animals.	
"	20th		Admitted 18 Animals. Evacuated 18 Animals. Capt Macfarlane reports from leave	
"	21st		Admitted 4 Animals. Evacuated 34 Animals.	
"	22nd		Admitted 17 Animals. Evacuated 25 Animals. Pte Bower proceeds on leave to U.K.	
"	23rd		Admitted 14 Animals. Evacuated 25 Animals.	
TROISVILLE	24th		Moved to TROISVILLE 9am to 10.30AM. Admitted 1 Animal. Evacuated 8 Animals.	
"	25th		Admitted 8 Animals. Evacuated 29 Animals. Pte Naylor reports back from leave	
MONTAY	26th		Moved to MONTAY 8.30AM to 10.30AM. Admitted 1 Animal. Evacuated 2 Animals.	
"	27th		Admitted 28 Animals. Evacuated 28 Animals.	
"	28th		Admitted 3 Animals. Evacuated 2 Animals	
"	29th		Admitted 14 Animals. Evacuated 16 Animals	
"	30th		Admitted 11 Animals. Evacuated 2 Animals	
"	31st		Admitted 9 Animals. Evacuated 10 Animals	

John Macfarlane
Capt. A.V.C.

CONFIDENTIAL.

WAR DIARY.

OF

O. C., 49th. MOBILE VETERINARY SECTION.

FROM

1st. NOVEMBER 1918.

TO

30th. NOVEMBER 1918.

(Volume XXXVI.)

John Macfarlane
Captain. A.V.C.
1st. December 1918.   Commanding, 49th. Mobile Vety. Section

Army Form C. 2118.

WAR DIARY
or
INTELLIGENCE SUMMARY.
(Erase heading not required.)

Instructions regarding War Diaries and Intelligence Summaries are contained in F. S. Regs., Part II. and the Staff Manual respectively. Title pages will be prepared in manuscript.

Place	Date Nov	Hour	Summary of Events and Information	Remarks and references to Appendices
MONTAY	1		Inspection of saddlery and harness. Admitted 3 animals. Evacuated 10 animals to No 5 V.E.S	YES
"	2		Inspection of Rifles and Respirators 09.00 parade. Pte MILLINER proceeds on leave.	
"	"		Admitted 6 animals Evacuated 1 animal to No 5 V.E.S	
"	3		A.D.V.S. V Corps visited Section. Admitted 15 animals Evacuated 16 animals to No 5 V.E.S	YES
"	4		Admitted 15 animals Evacuated 12 to No 5 V.E.S	
"	5		March to WAGNONVILLE. 09.30 to 13.00. S.S. HUGHES proceeds on leave Admitted Nil Evacuated Nil	YES
"	"		Evacuated 9 animals to No 5 V.E.S	
WAGNONVILLE	6		Admitted 3 animals, Evacuated Nil.	
"	7		Moved to ENGLEFONTAINE. 13.00 to 14.00 Admitted 6 animals Evacuated 3 animals to No 5 V.E.S	
ENGLEFONTAINE	8		Moved to LOCQUINOL. Admitted 24 animals. Evacuated 24 animals to No 5 V.E.S	
LOCQUINOL	9		A.D.V.S. V Corps visited Section. Inspection of Rifles and Respirators	
"	"		admitted 9 animals. Evacuated 4 animals to No 5 V.E.S	
"	10		Moved to AULNOYE 08.00 to 11.30. Admitted 6 animals. Evacuated 10 animals to No 5 V.E.S	
AULNOYE	11		News of Armistice received at 08.15. Pte BOWEN reports back from leave	
"	"		Admitted Nil. Evacuated Nil.	
"	12		Admitted 7 animals Evacuated Nil.	
"	13		Admitted 14 animals Evacuated 10 animals to No 5 V.E.S	

WAR DIARY or INTELLIGENCE SUMMARY.

Army Form C. 2118.

Place	Date	Hour	Summary of Events and Information	Remarks and references to Appendices
AULNOYE	14th Nov		Continued	
"	15	"	Admitted 7 animals Evacuated 14 to No 4 V.E.S	
"	16	"	Admitted 6 animals. Evacuated Nil.	
"	17	"	Inspection of Rifles at 09.00 parade Admitted 3 animals Evacuated 11 animals to No 4 V.E.S	
"	18	"	A.D.V.S.V Corp visited Section Admitted 4 animals, Evacuated 4 animals to No 4 S V.E.S	
"	19	"	Admitted 5 animals Evacuated 7 animals to No 4 V.E.S.	
"	19	"	Admitted 10 animals. Evacuated Nil.	
"	20	"	Admitted 1 animal Evacuated 15 animals to No 5 V.E.S	
"	21	"	Admitted 10 animals Evacuated 2 animals by Motor Ambulance to No 5 V.E.S	
"	22	"	Admitted 1 animal Evacuated 11 animals to No. 4 V.E.S Pte MILLINER report back from leave	
"	23	"	Admitted 1 animal. Evacuated Nil. Inspection of Rifles at 09.00 parade	
"	24	"	Admitted 7 animals Evacuated Nil.	
"	25	"	Admitted Nil Evacuated Nil. S.S. HUGHES reports back from leave	
"	26	"	Admitted 8 animals Evacuated 6 animals to No 4 V.E.S	
"	27	"	Admitted 5 animals Evacuated 2 animals by Motor Ambulance to No 5 V.E.S	

Army Form C. 2118.

WAR DIARY
or
INTELLIGENCE SUMMARY.
(Erase heading not required.)

Place	Date	Hour	Summary of Events and Information	Remarks and references to Appendices
AULNOYE	28" Nov		Continued Admitted 4 animals. Evacuated 10 animals to No 4 V.E.S	
"	29 "	"	Demobilisation of Coal miners. Druvis Edwards & Anthony	
"	"	"	A.S.C. (attached) proceeded to CAMBRAI. Admitted 3 animals. Evacuated Nil.	
"	30 "	"	Admitted 1 animals. Evacuated 5 animals to No. 4 V.E.S.	

John Macpherson
Capt. A.V.C.

49th MOBILE VETERINARY SECTION.
No.
Date 1/12/18

CONFIDENTIAL WAR DIARY

OF

CAPTAIN J MACFARLANE R.A.V.C.

49ᵗʰ MOBILE VETERINARY SECTION

VOL XXXVII

FROM DEC 1ˢᵗ 1918   TO DEC 31ˢᵗ 1918

Army Form C. 2118.

WAR DIARY
or
INTELLIGENCE SUMMARY.
(Erase heading not required.)

Instructions regarding War Diaries and Intelligence Summaries are contained in F.S. Regs., Part II. and the Staff Manual respectively. Title pages will be prepared in manuscript.

Place	Date	Hour	Summary of Events and Information	Remarks and references to Appendices
AULNOYE	DEC 1		Admitted 3 animals	
"	2		Admitted 3 animals. PTE TARREN leaves for examination as a Collier	
"	3		Admitted Nil. PTE NAYLOR admitted to Field Ambulance	
"	4		Admitted 4 animals	
"	5		Admitted 32 animals & evacuated 35 to IV VES	
"	6		Admitted 1 animal & evacuated 2 by Mtr Ambulance	
"	7		Admitted 5 animals. Inspection of Rifles & equipment	
"	8		Admitted 4 animals. PTE MARRIOTT proceed to UK on leave	
"	9		Admitted 7 animals & evacuated 8 to IV VES	
"	10		Admitted 3 animals. Cpl YALLOP proceed to UK on leave	
"	11		Admitted Nil. Moved from AULNOYE STN. to from WEST end of BERLIMONT	
BERLIMONT	12		Admitted 4 animals. PTE YOUNG admitted to 131 Field Ambulance	
"	13		Admitted Nil	
"	14		Admitted 4 animals. Inspection of Rifles & artillery	
"	15		Admitted 2 animals	

Army Form C. 2118.

WAR DIARY
or
INTELLIGENCE SUMMARY.
(Erase heading not required.)

Instructions regarding War Diaries and Intelligence Summaries are contained in F. S. Regs., Part II. and the Staff Manual respectively. Title pages will be prepared in manuscript.

Place	Date	Hour	Summary of Events and Information	Remarks and references to Appendices
BERLAIMONT	DEC 16		Admitted 3 animals	
"	" 17		Admitted 1 animal	
"	" 18		Admitted 4 animals	
"	" 19		Admitted 1 animal & evacuated 8 to XIII VES	
"	" 20		Admitted 1 animal	
"	" 21		Admitted 5 animals. Inspection of Horses, Harness & Vehicles	
"	" 22		Admitted 1 animal. MAJOR GAVIN D.A.D.V.S. proceeded to UK on leave, and O/C 49th Mobile Vetinary Section assumed duties	
"	" 23		Admitted 1 animal	
"	" 24		Admitted Nil	
"	" 25		Admitted Nil. General holiday observed	
"	" 26		Admitted 20 animals	
"	" 27		Admitted 1 animal & evacuated 19 to XIII VES & moved 9 rt	
"	" 28		Admitted 4 animals & evacuated 2 by XIII Corps Mtr Ambulance	
"	" 29		Admitted 1 animal	
"	" 30		Preparation for Move	
"	" 31		Moved from BERLAIMONT to NEUVILLE 08·00 to 15·00	

John Musprove
Capt RAVC
O/C 49 Mobile Vet Section

Confidential War Diary W8 39

of

Captain J. Macfarlane R.A.V.C.

49th Mobile Veterinary Section

Vol xxxvii

From Jan 1st 1919 To January 31st 1919

WAR DIARY or INTELLIGENCE SUMMARY

Army Form C. 2118.

Place	Date	Hour	Summary of Events and Information	Remarks and references to Appendices
NEUVILLY	January 1st 1919		Move from NEUVILLY to MASNIERS 08-00 to 15-00	
MASNIERS	2 "		Move from MASNIERS to MANANCOURT 07-15 to 15-00	
MANANCOURT	3 "		Move from MANANCOURT to MEAULTE 08-00 to 15-00 admitted 2 animals	
MEAULTE	4 "		Move from MEAULTE to LA HOUSSOYE 08-30 to 12-30 Cpl Yallop and Pte Marriott rejoined section from leave admitted 16 animals	
LA HOUSSOYE	5 "		A.D.V.S. 5th Corp. visits section Sergt Banks proceeds on leave to U.K. evacuated 19 animals to 5th V.E.S. at PICQUIGNY, admitted 5 animals	
"	6 "		admitted 26 animals	
"	7 "		admitted 2 animals evacuated 26 animals to 5 V.E.S men hard cases	
"	8 "		to proceed to ABBEVILLE with animals	
"	9 "		admitted 3 animals	
"	10 "		Routine as usual	
"	"		Pronl. Holt proceeds on leave to U.K. No 1029 Dvr Metcarine to relieve No 485 Sergt Munnully No 31478 Pte Kerrin arrives as reinforcement	
"	11 "		Inspection of Rifles & Box Respirators admitted 4 animals	
"	12 "		A.D.V.S. visited section No 485 Dvr Munnully proceed to LE HAVRE No 2 VET HOSPITAL 17 animals admitted	

Army Form C. 2118.

WAR DIARY
or
INTELLIGENCE SUMMARY.
(Erase heading not required.)

Instructions regarding War Diaries and Intelligence Summaries are contained in F.S. Regs. Part II. and the Staff Manual respectively. Title pages will be prepared in manuscript.

Place	Date	Hour	Summary of Events and Information	Remarks and references to Appendices
	January 1919			
LA HOUSSOYE	13	"	5 Animals admitted, 18 evacuated to No 5 V.E.S at PICQUIGNY	
"	14	"	4 animals admitted	
"	15	"	3 animals admitted	
"	16	"	2 animals admitted	
"	17	"	Inspection of Rifles and Equipment. 1 animal admitted	
"	18	"	1 animal admitted 2 animals to No 5 V.E.S PICQUIGNY	
"	19	"	1 animal admitted	
"	20	"	3 animals admitted	
"	21	"	11 animals admitted	
"	22	"	4 animals admitted 14 animals evacuated to No 5 V.E.S PICQUIGNY	
"	23	"	March from LA HOUSSOYE to ALLONVILLE 09.00 to 12.00 Sey Parker reported back from leave 2 animals admitted	
ALLONVILLE	24	"	8 Animals admitted	
"	25	"	Message received stating No 5 V.E.S PICQUIGNY closed. Inspection of Rifles and Box Respirators. 15 animals admitted 15 animals evacuated to 33 M.V.S at BREUIL	
"	26	"	4 animals admitted	

Army Form C. 2118.

WAR DIARY
or
INTELLIGENCE SUMMARY.
(Erase heading not required.)

Instructions regarding War Diaries and Intelligence Summaries are contained in F. S. Regs., Part II. and the Staff Manual respectively. Title pages will be prepared in manuscript.

Place	Date	Hour	Summary of Events and Information	Remarks and references to Appendices
		1919		
ALLONVILLE	27 January		6 Animals admitted	
"	28 "		4 animals admitted Pte Holt report back from leave	
"	29 "		3 animals admitted	
"	30 "			
"	31 "		1 animal admitted	

John Macfarlane
Capt. R.A.V.C.

Army Form C. 2118.

WAR DIARY
or
INTELLIGENCE SUMMARY.
(Erase heading not required.)

Place	Date	Hour	Summary of Events and Information	Remarks and references to Appendices
		1919		
ALLONVILLE	27 January		2 Animals admitted	
"	28 "		4 Animals admitted Pte Holt reported back from leave	
"	29 "		3 Animals admitted	
"	30 "			
"	31 "		1 Animal admitted	

John Macfarlane
Capt. R.A.V.C.

24
38

CONFIDENTIAL WAR DIARY

of

Captain J MACFARLANE RAVC

49th MOBILE VET SECTION

Vol XXXVIII

From Feby 1st 1919 to Feby 28th

Army Form C. 2118.

WAR DIARY
or
INTELLIGENCE SUMMARY.
(Erase heading not required.)

Instructions regarding War Diaries and Intelligence Summaries are contained in F. S. Regs., Part II. and the Staff Manual respectively. Title pages will be prepared in manuscript.

Place	Date	Hour	Summary of Events and Information	Remarks and references to Appendices
ALLONVILLE	1st February		3 Animals admitted. Inspection of Rifles and Equipment	
"	2nd		2 Animals admitted	
"	3rd		7 Animals admitted. 13 Animals evacuated to Nos.5 V.E.S PICQUIGNY	
"	4th		1 Animal admitted	
"	5th		1 Animal admitted	
"	6th		16 Animals admitted. 6 Animals evacuated to Nos.5 V.E.S PICQUIGNY	
"	7th		3 Animals admitted. 13 Animals evacuated to Nos.5 V.E.S PICQUIGNY	
"	8th		7 Animals admitted. Inspection of Rifles & Equipment	
"	9th		8 Animals admitted	
"	10th		2 Animals admitted	
"	11th		2 Animals admitted. 19 Animals evacuated to Nos.5 V.E.S PICQUIGNY	
"	12th		1 Animal admitted. 12 Animals evacuated to Nos.5 V.E.S PICQUIGNY	
"	13th		Routine as usual	
"	14th		8 Animals admitted. 4 Animals evacuated to Nos.5 V.E.S PICQUIGNY	
"	15th		11 Animals admitted. Inspection of Rifles & Box Respirators	

WAR DIARY
or
INTELLIGENCE SUMMARY.
(Erase heading not required.)

Army Form C. 2118.

Place	Date	Hour	Summary of Events and Information	Remarks and references to Appendices
ALLONVILLE	16th Febry		4 Animals admitted	
"	17th "		4 Animals admitted	
"	18th "		3 Animals admitted	
"	19th "		1 Animal admitted 8 Animals evacuated to No 5 V.E.S PICQUIGNY	
"	20th "		2 Animals admitted Inspection of Rifles and equipment	
"	21st "		2 Animals admitted	
"	22nd "		1 Animal admitted A.D.V.S 5th Corps visits Section	
"	23rd "		16 Animals admitted Routine as usual	
"	24th "		25 Animals admitted	
"	26th "		2 Animals admitted 21 Animals evacuated for Destruction 5 Animals evacuated for Sale at AMIENS	
"	26th "		2 Animals admitted 6 Animals evacuated to No 5 V.E.S MONTIERES for Destruction	
"	27th "		168 Animals admitted 150 Animals prepared for Sale at AMIENS	
"	28th "		1 Animal admitted, attended sale of animals at AMIENS	
			Sold 199 from 5 V.E.S and 149 from 49th M.V.S	

John Mapleton
Capt RAVC

90

Vol 41 3F

CONFIDENTIAL WAR DIARY

OF

CAPTAIN J MACFARLANE RAVC

49TH MOBILE VETERINARY SECTION

FROM MARCH 1ST 1919. Vol XXXIX TO MARCH 31ST

WAR DIARY
or
INTELLIGENCE SUMMARY.

(Erase heading not required)

Army Form C. 2118.

Place	Date	Hour	Summary of Events and Information	Remarks and references to Appendices
ALLONVILLE (SOMME)	Month			
	1		Admitted 3 animals	
"	2		Admitted 1 animal	
"	3		Admitted 12 animals. 1 Sutler Horse to Boiveler for upholstie to U.K. Pte PITSON demobilized	
"	4		Admitted 1 animal	
"	5		Admitted 175 animals. O/C & Sutler engaged in classifying, branding & marking in preparation for Sale	
"	6		Admitted 180 animals. Remainder of Sale animals classified & branded.	
"	7		Sale at AMIENS of 353 'SURPLUS I' animals conducted by O/C 49 M V S	
"	8		Admitted 1 animal	
"	9		Admitted 4 animals	
"	10		Admitted 5 animals	
"	11		Admitted 53 animals. O/C & Sutler engaged in classifying, branding & preparation for Sale	
"	12		Admitted 2 animals. Sale at Corbie of 50 animals conducted by O/C 49 M V S	
"	13		Admitted 150 animals. O/C & Sutler engaged in classifying, branding & preparation for Sale	
"	14		Admitted 150 animals. Remainder of Sale animals classified & branded	
"	15		Sale at AMIENS of 300 animals conducted by O/C 49 M V S	
"	16		Cpl YALLOP leave for Demobilization	
"	17		Admitted 2 animals, evacuated 4 to No 5 V E S	

Army Form C. 2118.

WAR DIARY
or
INTELLIGENCE SUMMARY.
(Erase heading not required.)

Instructions regarding War Diaries and Intelligence Summaries are contained in F.S. Regs., Part II. and the Staff Manual respectively. Title pages will be prepared in manuscript.

Place	Date	Hour	Summary of Events and Information	Remarks and references to Appendices
ALLONVILLE (SOMME)	18		Admitted 2 animals. 1 Destroyed	
	19		Admitted 2 animals.	
	20		Admitted 103 animals. Section engaged in branding in preparation for Sale	
			Collected proceeds of Sale on 15th inst. & paid to Field Cashier	
	21		Sale at AMIENS of 106 animals, conducted by O/C #97 VS	
	22		New arrival of suspensor of Demobilization	
	23		Admitted 2 animals	
	24		Admitted 4 animals	
	25		Issued 2 animals to 267 POW Co. 1 Destroyed. 2 Evacuated to No 5 VES	
	26		CAPT. J. CULHANE taken over Section. Cpl BOND demobilized.	
			PTE BARTHOLOMEW Leave to UK. Admitted 2 animals. Evacuated 14 to 5 VES	
	27		Admitted 1 animal & Evacuated to No 5 VES. 1 Returned to Unit (Cured)	
	28		Admitted No 1. PTE LITTLE to UK for demobilization. PTE WEBSTER Leave to UK	
	29		Moved to QUERRIEU 09-30 to 13-30. Admitted 1 animal	
	30		CAPT. J. CULHANE hands over & assumes Section. Orders received from	
			ADVS, 4th DADVS, for reduction of Section to Cadre strength	
	31		Remaining 7 animals (in charge) dispatched to No 5 VES. PTE HOLT dispatched	
			to No 5 VES (Surplus) —— Section now at Cadre Strength	

John Macfarlane
Capt. RAVC

A 3834 Wt. W4973/M687. 750,000. 8/16 D.D. & L. Ltd. Forms/C.2118/13.

WAR DIARY or INTELLIGENCE SUMMARY

Army Form C. 2118.

May 1919 45ᵗʰ Mob. Vety. Sectⁿ

M⁻ 3 Army FRANCE

Vol 4-B

Place	Date	Hour	Summary of Events and Information	Remarks and references to Appendices
Montières	1		Took over animals & equipment from 49 M.V.S., 36 animals. Ambulance & supply waggon men to complete 49 M.V.S.	
	2		Ambulance truck from Peronne. 1 Ambulance sent to Rainville for River. Sgt Worsington & Pte Crane returned from leave. Sent in 2 Bullock Cars to Abbeville (1075.50 po). Ambulance to Rainville and Corbie. B/66 Pastor Player Pritman 1 called. Ambulance with 2 drivers sent to Bouzy at Cerisy (Gondrin) Pte Cook & Davies despatched to Cambrai for detachment work	
	3		Ambulance to Doullens and Arcis to station. Pte Sheppard & Bernard for ambulance duty to Doullens	
	4		Sgt Porter R.A.V.C. sent to Sittbosps Concentration camp for Demob. Ambulance returned from Doullens, River & Cerisy duty. Ambulance to Amiens	
	5		Ambulance to Rainville & Cerisy "B" buster cases sent to Abattoirs (1680. co/po) Sgt Easton	
	6		R.M.C. called reported	
	7		2 Bullock Wagons to Abattoirs (925 fr) Ambulance to Workshop. Ambulance to Cerisy & Trincourt l'Abbé	
	8		Ambulance to Rainville, visited 53 L.G, 111 G.L.G, 141 Chinese Co, 135 Lab Co, 188 P.O.W, 189 Pow, 253 POW, 254 Pow, Argt Road attacks, 3AAHT and 17 Police Amien Corps. Edmonds Eccurt.	

Army Form C. 2118.

WAR DIARY
or
INTELLIGENCE SUMMARY.
(Erase heading not required.)

May 1919.   2

Place	Date	Hour	Summary of Events and Information	Remarks and references to Appendices
Montières	9		Ambulance weigh 2 horses to Albertville (M.V.H.) Casualty of Mules to Candas A.C.C. # Butcher Cases sent to Amiens. (2167-50 fs)	
	10		Capt Jones left for England. Followed several animals that have not appear to have been done lately.	
	11		Ambulance to Amiens	
	12		Capt Lohman called. Ambulance to Picauville and Boves. Visited 189 and 301 P.O.W. Camps. M.T. Driver Taylor reported for duty from 3rd K.R.R.	
	13		Ambulance to Amiens. Sent 2 animals to Puchevilliers (345 fs) Pte Ross left for U.K. leave. Visited at S.A.P.M. and Base Cashier. Ambulance motor to evacuate for mule. Horsed Ambulance to Glisy for mule. Evacuated 11 Cavalry Cases to Candas C.C.C. one mule sent to Butcher (660 fs)	
	14		Ambulance to Courcellette (nr Bapaume) 47 kilos for a sick Ambulance to Amiens with 1 Butcher case (660 fs) Capt Edwards called. 62 visited 53 Lab Group, 111 Chinese Lab. Coy. 3rd Aust T.C. Field Ambulance 223 P.O.W. 189 P.O.W. 122 Bde & 123 Bde R.F.A. 461 & 2 Lester D.A.C. Glisy and	✓
	15			

Army Form C. 2118.

WAR DIARY
or
INTELLIGENCE SUMMARY.
(Erase heading not required.)

May 1919.

Place	Date	Hour	Summary of Events and Information	Remarks and references to Appendices
Frontiers	15		Infantry at Clairy.	
	16		Ambulance to Dorgnies (4 P.O.W.) to collect cases from Curlu. Sent a driver to Blangy-Tronville to obtain a mules tooth.	
	17		3 Animals to Barleux (2 horses + 1 mule) (2122-50 Frs). Ambulance to Proyart.	
	18		Took 2 horses to Capt. Hatfield. Ambulance to Marieux and Péronne.	
	19		Ambulance to Villers-Bretonneux. Visited 252 P.O.W. and Greek boy. Sent driver to Bonnay to Vacant Horse. Pte Hall sent on leave to U.K.	
	20		Ambulance to Proyart and Amiens. Called to See 3002 horses to Lignerolles Café. Sent 2 horses Hatfield (1102 Frs).	
	21		Ambulance to Bouzdon and L'Étoile.	
	22		Evacuated 1 Horse and 5 mules to Sandown. Ambulance to Amiens Station. Sent 5 Brethers Cases to Abbattoir (3975 Francs).	

Army Form C. 2118.

WAR DIARY
or
INTELLIGENCE SUMMARY.
(Erase heading not required.)

4 May 1919.

Place	Date	Hour	Summary of Events and Information	Remarks and references to Appendices
Morterers	23		Ambulance to Poulainville hallowed animals in Pocken & Hospital	
	24		Ambulance to Amiens. Capt Lukman called.	
			Butcher crose to Abattoir (675-Fo)	
	25		Ambulance force to Poulainville	
	26		Ambulance to Sourieux. Pte Mostin proceeded to U.K. on leave	
			one Butcher coise to abattoir (697-50 Fo) Col. Pellin called	
	27		Ambulance to Amiens & Flaucy Trouille	
	28		Ambulance to Candas Showed 9 Hoses	
			2 Butcher cows to abattoir (732-50 Fo)	
	29		Ambulance to Berlin for Police Horse. Capt Bowden called. The Best	
			Returned from U.K. Visited 20th P.O.W. & Aust. Frene Detch. 8 Butcher cows to Abattoir (2037 Fo)	
	30		Ambulance to Candas. Showed 14 animals to Section S+D.V.S. Called and Capt Bowden	
			Pte Roux sent to Flixecourt on Temporary duty	
	31		Left for Boulogne and Calais at 9. Capt Bowden arrived to carry on in	
			my absence. 3 Butcher cows to Abattoir (1531-25 Fo)	

Subject:- War Diary.

O.C.,
49th M.V.S.

Reference attached.

If still required, this document should be sent direct to G.H.Q., as heretofore. Please note.

H.Q.,
No. 3 Area.
7/8/19.

T. Lishman, Major,
D.A.D.V.S. NO. 3 AREA.

Army Form C. 2118.

40th MOBILE VETERINARY SECTION.

WAR DIARY
or
INTELLIGENCE SUMMARY
(Erase heading not required.)

Date: June 1919.

Instructions regarding War Diaries and Intelligence Summaries are contained in F.S. Regs., Part II. and the Staff Manual respectively. Title pages will be prepared in manuscript.

49th M.V.S.

8 JUL 1919

Place	Date	Hour	Summary of Events and Information	Remarks and references to Appendices
Montieres	June 1		Routine Work.	
"	2	=	Ambulance to Flexicourt with Capt. Coombs & self. Routine. Evacuated 6 Riders to Cauderes.	
"	3	=	Ambulance to Flexicourt attend D.A.D.V.S. & V.O's office. Examined dog that had bitten French child. Gen. De Roqueney called. Capt. Coombs to Cambrai. Capt. Scott S.C. carry on as V.O.i/c Sub Area. Pte Dyson W.R.A.673 exit for temporary duty, to Doullens Sub Area.	
		=	Evacuate 11 animals to Cauderes. Sent 2 animals to Abattoir.	
	4	=	Ambulance to Flexicourt, attend D.A.D.V.S. & V.O. office. ½ Day for the men to celebrate Kings Birthday. Gen De Roqueney's charger sent in for scissor clipping. Ambulance to Hangest for M.P. Horse.	
	5	=	Pte Innes return from leave. Sgt Lenster Y 20106 & Pte Crise S.C. 31665 arrive from 13 V.H. for duty. Cpl Heathcotes 24182 proceeded on leave from Cambrai to U.K. 3-6-19. 26985 Pte Sheppard reports fit duty from Doullens. 20180 Pte Bolland F. return from Cav. to St. Quentin. Ambulance Flexicourt Ambulance to Amiens Twice. Rtn Beacon Cambrai Sub Area return from leave.	

WAR DIARY
or
INTELLIGENCE SUMMARY
(Erase heading not required.)

Army Form C. 2118
2
June 1919

Place	Date	Hour	Summary of Events and Information	Remarks and references to Appendices
Montreux	June 6		D.A.D.V.S. inspected Camp. Received Waggon load of horses from Peronne Rem. Area.	
	" 7		25412 Pte Davies H. back off leave 27/6/19.	
			Ambulance twice to Slivry. Brought 4 mules. Horse Ambulance to Slivry.	
	" 8		15244 S/S. Day to U.K. for Leave 4/6/19.	
			Camp Hdqrs Lines Inspection. 9 horses & drivers failed for night en route for Harcourt.	
	" 9		Routine work. Gave men a half a day. Received Hides (small cut) from Arrotal Grave Detach.	
	" 10		Mallieu all animals in section lines & Hospital Bretteres 189 P.O.W. Animals.	
			Ambulance to Longeau with men & luggage of leave. Leave of 70 S.V.B.L.	
	" 11		to Longeau for Entraining. D.A.D.R. inspected. Had Foot-Bar. visited Several units.	
			8 Animals to Canada.	
	" 12		Sent Serg. & Party, to Canada to draw 12 Mules.	
			Col. Pullin called on Rumieroy in passing. 22673. Pte Tyser. J.A. to U.K for leave.	
	" 13		Evacuated 14.(including 12 L.D) for England to Canada. Ambulance to Canada.	
			D.A.D.R Called.	
	" 14		Ambulance to St Quentin & Albert. D.A.D.V.S. called & inspected.	
	" 15		Ambulance to Harcourt. Took instructions from Col. Pullin. Office Routine.	
			Waggons sent to 5 Corps Concert Camp. Ambulance to Vergnement to America.	

WAR DIARY
or
INTELLIGENCE SUMMARY.
(Erase heading not required.)

Army Form C. 2118.

3/ June 1919.

Place	Date	Hour	Summary of Events and Information	Remarks and references to Appendices
Monteres	June 16	—	Ambulance to Heriacourt & Amiens. Pte Stone to V.K. on leave. Pte Stopforde to V.K. on leave.	
	" 17	—	Notified Major Lickman at Headquarters of Capt Brookes. Pte Martin & Dr. Watson admitted to Hospital.	
	—	—	Ambulance to Heriacourt & Amiens. Funeral of Horses from Peronne. D.A.D.V.S. called. 4 Batches Cases to Abancourt. 1 S/Sergt 1 Sergt & 33 O.Rs arrived from 70th V.H. Calais	
	" 18	—	Ambulance to Amiens. Sent Dr Sieman to Doullens with liver prior to embarkation on Thursday at Candas.	
	" 19	—	Pte Rowe "sports" from Heavcourt for Duty. Visited Lingen, Bonin, Flixy, Plenzy, Liencelle, Villies Bretto, Vaux, & Montieres. Also inspected units & clearing Horses & Mules. 3 forces Mules arrived from Boman.	
	" 20	—	Ambulance to Doullens for Stores. Pte Hill reported for duty from 70th V.H. Calais. Pte Tallant proceeded on leave to U.K. Capt Featherstone returned from U.K. leave from train.	
	" 21	—	Ambulance to Tyrnetta (Albert) for Horse. Capt Trouvile called en route for Peronne.	
	" 22	—	Ambulance to Lamotte. Capt Calvert & Paxton Park called from Canada.	
	" 23	—	Ambulance to Flixy & Heavcourt. Dr Walker Pte S.C.M.T. reported for Duty from St.V.R.P.	

Army Form C. 2118.

WAR DIARY
or
INTELLIGENCE SUMMARY.
(Erase heading not required.)

June 1919.

Instructions regarding War Diaries and Intelligence Summaries are contained in F. S. Regs., Part II. and the Staff Manual respectively. Title pages will be prepared in manuscript.

Place	Date	Hour	Summary of Events and Information	Remarks and references to Appendices
Montières	June 24.	—	Ambulance to Amiens twice, & Flixicourt. Visited Base Cashier, & formed them closed on M/c of Peace Celebrations. A/S. Sgt. returned from Leave in U.K.	
"	25	—	Pte Asket & Pte Doug left for leave to U.K.	
"	26	—	Pte Olive left for leave in U.K. Ambulance to Poulainville & Flixicourt.	
"	27	—	Ambulance to Amiens & Corbie. Horse Ambulance to Amiens for tow from 119 Labo. Coy. D.A.V.S. called. Capt. Cranito called. 2 Lieut. Capt. Boys Wotherspoon & two R.A.S.C. men sent in place of same. Agreed to return two lorries of the Grave Company. Pte Yeager on leave to U.K. Chaston exchanged for Pte. Burnett. R.A.V.C.	
"	28	—	Pte. Burnett, S. proceed on Leave to U.K. 2 whole holiday for the men. Ambulance to Amiens with 2 butcher cases.	
"	29	—	Ambulance to Hay & Rue to collect horses.	
"	30.	—	Ambulance to Amiens, Breton Springs. Lettres to Abattoirs.	

Richard Scott T
Corpl RWC
O.C 49 M.V.S

Army Form C. 2118.

49th MOBILE VETERINARY SECTION.
No. 9
Date July 1919

Vol 45

WAR DIARY
or
INTELLIGENCE SUMMARY.
(Erase heading not required.)

Instructions regarding War Diaries and Intelligence Summaries are contained in F. S. Regs., Part II. and the Staff Manual respectively. Title pages will be prepared in manuscript.

Place	Date	Hour	Summary of Events and Information	Remarks and references to Appendices
Fravieres	1		Ambulance to Cambrai. Pte Ross killed. Innocent & Chalciaux to Cambrai. Pte Barrett from Cambrai	
	2		Received 13 Base allotments for July. Pte Tyner & Stan returned from UK. Pte Hamilton proceeded to UK on leave.	
	4		Ambulance to Cambrai & Amiens. Sent on exchange horses for & for Z. DDVS & DADVS called & inspected	
	5		Ambulance to Cambrai. Pte Hunter returned from hospital. Received smile heavier heavier cart from N25 Company by Pte Rose provisions lorry	
	6		Pte Ross killed. Ambulance to Picardie. Pte Ronse to Ronsse	
	7		Pte Benne to Ronsse. Pte sent to St Quentin. Cpl Beare, Pte Ross killer, Ambulance to Cambrai	
	8		Ambulance to Amiens. Pte Innocent proceed on leave	
	9		Barbers amalgamated with Cavalry Ambulance to Amiens. Pte Ronse proceed on leave to UK. Cpl Barker from Hosp. DADVS called & inspected	25

WAR DIARY or INTELLIGENCE SUMMARY

Army Form C. 2118

No. 10
Date July 1919
Unit: 49th Mobile Veterinary Section

Place	Date	Hour	Summary of Events and Information	Remarks and references to Appendices
Frontières	10		Ambulance to Dourlers. Col Nadorff arrived (Regimental Officer). Pte Rupp proceeds on duty. Pte Tallows arrived from St Quentin. Pte Rowe & Capt Scott's grooms arrived with 2 chargers. Camp inspected by Section Offr.	
	11		Ambulance to Potteville. Pte Healy to U.K. on leave. Pte Hartwater reported for duty from 30th M.V.S. Visit from General Greaves (Remounts Inspector General)	
	12		Ambulance to Dourlers & Pervins. Pte Eisen from leave. SDR visits issued.	
	13		Pte Bennett to leave. Pte Tallows to N.9 & V.H. Pte Krieger from leave.	
	14		Ambulance returned from Pervins. S.M.O. 3rd Army inspected unit. General Holroyd for Troops Inn. had a fancy dress pageant. Arrives	
	15		Ambulance to Avines.	
	16		Pte Bennett from leave. Capt Inv. boards arrived from Pervins. Sub Area with ordinary for empty duty. Pte Hoelker to Hosp. Ambulance & Workshops for repairs	5.
	17		St Taylor RASC MT. Stores. Depts. Leave prisoners on leave to UK. Ambulance to St Jérôme. 2 LIT. Arrival at Gosbrai. Graphicals with Ambulance 18 22.M.M. Bugton Park & strength off & strength	

Army Form C. 2118.

46th MOBILE VETERINARY SECTION.
No. 11
Date July 1919.

WAR DIARY
or
INTELLIGENCE SUMMARY.
(Erase heading not required.)

Instructions regarding War Diaries and Intelligence Summaries are contained in F. S. Regs., Part II. and the Staff Manual respectively. Title pages will be prepared in manuscript.

Place	Date	Hour	Summary of Events and Information	Remarks and references to Appendices
Hortues	18		Ambulance to Rennes & Albert by Hanvale RASC MT Column	
	19		Demurria renders from Rennes Lt-aven Ambulance to Railhead	
			Horse Ambulance rising for Troops	
	20		Offr. Hacker to have Lohemond RTO orders no entry no result Rennes sub-area	
	21		1 sick animal from Rennes sub-area Visit from MO Ambulance one to every three horses posting to Ambulance for Trucks Army Ambulance to 119 Column to N.Albert	
	22		RASC called & ordered to register 96 Bonnets on loan to UK Offr Hacker on return from leave Gun 1372-25 fa to Base Ambulance	QS
			brought c/Lt Howarth to Ambulance	
	23		Offr. Hacker proceeded home to UK Offr Sheppard from leave	
	24		Visit Bristton Ambulance to 113 Column Co	
	25		Visit Ambulance Ambulance to railway	
	26		Offr Davies returns reported from Rennes Sub-area	
	27		to Royle RASC MT Column	

WAR DIARY
or
INTELLIGENCE SUMMARY.
(Erase heading not required.)

Army Form C. 2118.

Place	Date	Hour	Summary of Events and Information	Remarks and references to Appendices
Juvincourt	28		Visited abattoir. Ambulance to Flavigny.	
	29		Visited abattoir. SADVS called. Pte Barrett from leave. Pte Hartley proceeded on leave to UK	
	30		Card Corpse 22576-25/7. Receipts for ammo sold to Butcher Corps. Lm Cornish promoted to No 114 Vet. Hosp. Abbeville. Ambulance to Aizincourt & No 14 Vety. Hosp. Pte Lowe & Murphy from leave.	
	31		SADVS called. Cpl Featherstone, Pte Tuitten, Smith, & Dent from Command.	

Richard Scott Capt. RAVC
OC 112 M.V.S.

www.ingramcontent.com/pod-product-compliance
Lightning Source LLC
Chambersburg PA
CBHW081530160426
43191CB00011B/1728